"The U-boat attack was our worst evil
Winston Churchill

"The Battle of the Atlantic was the dom   ᵒ ιαςτor all through
the war. Never for one moment could we forget that everything
happening elsewhere, on land, at sea, or in the air, depended
ultimately on its outcome, and amid all other cares we viewed its
changing fortunes day by day with hope and apprehension. "

"By April 1944 the Battle of the Atlantic had been decisively won.
Our scientists had been shouldering detection problems as their
contribution to the enormous Navy effort.....today's only effective
detector of submerged submarines –SONAR".
Lt. Cdr. A.P. Hilar, USN, Naval Department Office of the Chief
of Naval Operations, Washington DC 1946

Eric Alexander was born in South Africa in 1916. He came to England in
1939 prior to the start of the Second World War. On gaining his
doctorate at Oxford University in 1941 he joined the Admiralty as an
Experimental Officer working on anti-submarine detection devices. After
the war he made his career with the Admiralty as a sonar scientist in a
Dorset Establishment. In 1966 he was seconded to the diplomatic service
of the Foreign Office and appointed Scientific Councellor to the British
Embassy in Moscow.

Dr. Eric Alexander, 1945

20·V·2023

Sound of the Waves

For my darling grand-daughter,
Emily,

A WWII story about your
great-grandfather, Eric,
with lots of love from
Grandma hibley
xx x xx

(previously Elizabeth. A. Alexander)

Sound of the Waves

A WW2 MEMOIR
How sonar scientists worked
to defeat the U-boat threat.

E.A. Alexander

LIBERTY
BOOKS

ISBN 978 1 5272 6290 4

Image retouching Bruce Wallace

Liberty Books
11 Granville Road, Sevenoaks
Kent TN13 1EX

www.sound-of-the-waves.com

To my son, Toby

Contents

Acknowledgement

Very many books and articles available online – extensive and wide-ranging - were consulted whilst researching this memoir both to clarify and verify scientific facts regarding anti-submarine detection devices and to check historical war time events. Admiralty Papers available at the National Archives, Kew have been very useful as has the list of some of the (Unclassified) Internal Reports 1942-1951 written by Dr. Alexander and found in his papers at the time of his death.

The book regarded as the official history on research into underwater acoustics, *Seek & Strike; sonar, anti-submarine warfare and the Royal Navy 1914-1954.* (Hackman, HMSO Books, 1984), is a wide ranging and scholarly examination of the subject. This book was an invaluable resource for which I am very grateful. However, throughout my life – and in the process of researching this biographical memoir - I had the benefit of hearing first-hand my parents' memories of their time at Her Majesty's Anti-Submarine Experimental Establishment in Fairlie, Scotland (HM A/SEE) and it was therefore possible when writing to expand and clarify a few facts mentioned in the text and notes of the aforementioned book.

Grateful thanks must also go to those who so diligently and kindly read my drafts, those who advised on specific areas of production and those whose design input was invaluable. If I have omitted any names, not given credit where it was due, or recorded events or research in the incorrect order, my apologies.

The majority of photographs reproduced in this book were taken by Eric Alexander – and the copyright remains with the author – unless otherwise credited or noted. Postcards shown are contemporaneous. Whilst every effort has been made to trace copyright holders of some uncredited photographic images, where this has not been possible (whilst appreciating that the copyright remains with the original owner) I apologise and will be very pleased to insert the appropriate acknowledgement in subsequent printings or to remove the image.

Preface

E.A. Alexander, yes, our names sound the same, my father's and mine, but the story is his. *Sound of the Waves* is my father's account of his feelings and circumstances and describes events as he recounted them since WWII as to how Asdic – sonar - scientists worked in secret for the British Admiralty to refine and develop anti-submarine detection equipment in order to defeat the German U-boats that threatened to starve Britain into submission, to develop the equipment used in the 'X' Craft miniature submarines to attack the German battleship, KMS *Tirpitz*, and in the craft that took part in the D-Day landings.

My father had a brain haemorrhage aged 78 and to help him recover I encouraged him to talk of his childhood in South Africa, his study at Oxford and early working life in Scotland on the basis that early memories are often more easily accessed for the elderly than recent events. His determination to recover was prodigious and he followed all the medical advice given but I like to think that delving into what he had achieved and experienced in his early life helped the process of recovery.

To hear him speak of his time with the Admiralty during WWII made me aware of how little we know of – and how little we appreciate - the scientific and technical work and the lives of the men and women who carried it out behind the scenes in secret establishments. They may not have been physically at risk in combat on behalf of their country but without their creativity and endeavour to produce and perfect the equipment that was installed in submarines, ships and auxiliary craft the lives of many who sailed in them would have been lost.

In writing the story I wanted to show - through my father's eyes and as much as possible in his words - not only the scientific and technical achievements but also that these scientists were not simply some of 'Churchill's army of boffins' working in a vacuum but were ordinary people with families and interests outside of their fields of study. In doing so, getting a balance between the personal aspect of my father's background and experience and the technical aspect of the scientific facts has tested my ingenuity. To the greatest extent I have relied on my father's verbal stories – often referring to his wife, my late mother, for clarification - and on taped and transcribed conversations we had over the years but I have had to assemble many of the scientific details that my father did not divulge through detective work in order to join the dots and fill the gaps. My parents had both signed the Official Secrets Act and never mentioned highly classified information whilst keeping diaries and taking photographs of sensitive subjects were prohibited.

However, the unclassified Admiralty reports my father wrote - found in his papers at the time of his death - have been of great use when verifying the time line and extent of his research. His verbal scientific observations on anti-submarine detection research and devices and his experiences have been checked wherever possible whilst sensitive experiments and research work he kept confidential have been investigated and expounded as far as I am able by referring to the many books and papers that refer to Asdic sets and submarine domes published since WWII or those available at the National Archives.

Scientific facts regarding anti-submarine detection and warfare during the war have been released in many publications since 1945 with some previously classified facts now available to be seen under the 50 – and now 70 - year rule. However, my father's final posting as Scientific Councellor to the British Embassy in Moscow in 1966 has meant that most references to Dr. Eric Alexander and his highly confidential and often top secret work for the Admiralty since 1941 have not been available for inspection or have been redacted in publications for security reasons which has posed a considerable challenge whilst researching this book.

Notwithstanding, this memoir contains a very personal account of the life and research of a young scientist and his colleagues working in a secret establishment in Scotland during WWII to help defeat the threat of the U-boat and improve detection devices for other craft and situations and many of the intimate and specific details mentioned within have never been made known until now.

The Firth of Clyde

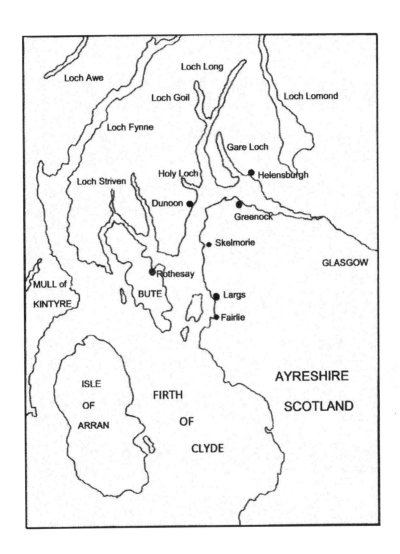

Loch Awe
Loch Long
Loch Goil
Loch Lomond
Loch Fynne
Gare Loch
Holy Loch
Loch Striven
Helensburgh
Dunoon
Greenock
Skelmorie
GLASGOW
MULL of
KINTYRE
Rothesay
BUTE
Largs
Fairlie

ISLE
OF
ARRAN

FIRTH

OF

CLYDE

AYRESHIRE

SCOTLAND

Sound of the Waves

1. This is London: July 1939

Postcard of Piccadilly Circus, London

It's mayhem. I love it. Red buses, black cabs, bicycles, lorries, motor cars. Noise and fumes. People everywhere, crowding the pavements, crossing the road, standing outside cinemas, queuing outside fishmongers. Boys selling newspapers, girls selling flowers, men calling out their wares. The dumpy barrage balloons wobbling overhead and the sandbags stacked up against basement windows below look like preparations for war have been well made. The balloons must be to force German bombers to fly higher and the sandbags are obviously placed to protect against blast. Apart from that everything else seems to be operating as usual. Offices are open, shops are selling, buses running.

Fresh off our Union Castle ship my mother and I check into The Regent Palace Hotel. It's a new hotel on the same site as the one we used to stay in so we feel quite at home. Seven pounds six shillings a night. We're right on Piccadilly Circus. In the thick of it. Compared to home I have never seen people so over-relaxed: chatting, hanging around in groups, joking, men smoking, women shopping, gossiping. I thought everyone would be in the depths of depression. The threat of war hanging over them. But the young women are all dolled up in their summer frocks and high heels. The men all talking about cricket. I love it.

My mother asks me to accompany her to Barclays Bank in Cockspur Street where she has money deposited and now deposits some more, retrieved from under the flap at the bottom of her Innovation trunk. Then it's back to the hotel where the telephone is in constant use as she contacts her friends, makes appointments at the hairdressing salon and plans visits to fashion emporia. But I spend these first days simply walking about. On up Regent Street I go. Down the Mall. I saunter through Soho and linger outside the food and wine shops along Old Compton and Brewer Streets.

The risqué adverts for the theatre in Great Windmill Street are a source of amusement and I search for the salt-beef sandwich bar Dad liked to eat at. The one with the photographs of boxers on the wall. Grapes from a market stall don't seem fresh but nothing dampens my enthusiasm. I get invitations from tarts and suspicious looks from spivs. London is thrilling.

Along Shaftesbury Avenue the theatres are blacked out but I scan all the bills. People file in to see the shows, their gas masks in little cardboard boxes on string over their shoulders as if it's quite the natural thing to carry such an awkward package on a day out. Wandering around Bloomsbury I look into all the bookshops and buy a postcard of Piccadilly and another of Oxford Circus. Then venturing into the city I am impressed by the imposing office buildings, gummed brown paper taped over their windows.

Taking the tube to quiet Bayswater I find where we stayed all those years ago. Then back through the parks, less beautiful now, the grass gone, trenches dug across them for shelter in case of falling bombs. Lunch is in an Italian café, beer in a crowded pub. Over the Thames by one bridge and back across another. I get my bearings, find my way about. Most importantly, I go right down the Strand and locate Kings College. What a time I'm going to have here.

But on the Monday morning, when I turn up to enrol as a post-graduate, not everything looks quite right. There are an awful lot of people walking in and out of the university buildings with boxes. Men in overalls are stacking them on the pavement, piling them into lorries. Taking a deep breath in I go. 'Can you tell me where the Faculty of Science is, please?' I ask. 'Down the hall, up those stairs, at the end.' Passing along the passages office doors are open, desks are being cleared, bookcases emptied. I make enquiries.

'Sorry, there's nobody here', I am told. 'We're decamping. London is vulnerable. If there's a bomb we could lose all our research. We're off lock, stock and barrel'. 'Off? Where?' I ask in horror and get told, 'Bristol.' I am in shock. 'Bristol?' I repeat, like a dimwit. 'Yes, Kings College, London, is going to Bristol for the foreseeable future'. I pull out my letter from Professor Denison in South Africa. Point out that he has written to the Dean of the Faculty of Science. Show them that I am expected. That I am to study Chemical Kinetics for my PhD. 'Sorry', they say, 'we can't help'.

I have travelled all the way from South Africa to go to Kings College, London. London, not Bristol. My mother has sold our house, sold the furniture, sold everything. She's left the Cape to see me realise my dream of doing research at Kings College, London. My dream of gaining a PhD at Kings College, London. But now the research department is packing up and moving out. I am so stunned I have to sit down. Right there on the nearest lab stool.

What *am* I going to *do*. I try to make an appointment to see the Dean, hoping and praying that there is some mistake. 'The Dean will not be available,' I am informed. 'What about the Professor of Chemistry?' I ask in desperation. Yes, they will arrange it. I walk back towards Piccadilly Circus trying very hard not to let my disappointment engulf me. I need to compose myself before breaking the news to my mother.

She has only come because she wants to live in London. With me. She explodes when I tell her. It doesn't help.

She and I turn up at the appointed hour the next day. After the usual pleasantries I say, 'I want to study in London. It is essential for me to do my research here. I can't do it in Bristol. I need facilities'. 'Sorry', says the Professor. 'The department is packing up. We'll come back as soon as we know it's all over. All Clear. Have you thought of Oxford? They have an excellent postgraduate chemistry department. They may have room for you there. I can write. Recommend you'.

My mother is only interested in living in London but I point out that it's no longer an option. That Oxford is closer to London than Bristol. She grudgingly agrees that it might be the only solution. We accept the Professor's offer of help and decide to visit Dad's sisters while we wait to find out where I can work on my thesis. *If* I can work on my thesis. *If* Oxford will have me. But I am miserable. Kings is what I have beavered away at my studies for. What I have given up fun and games for. What I have travelled from South Africa to England for. I am sunk in despondency. The bloom of my new life has well and truly worn off.

The East End and London West One. Cheap or chic. Chalk or cheese. That's the enormous difference between them. Two quite different worlds. Most of her life my grandmother Rosenthal lived in Whitechapel in the East End. She was born there, in Spitalfields. It didn't matter if they were educated or illiterate, it's where most refugees like Dad's grandparents ended up a hundred years ago when they escaped from Poland. They had left everything behind and times were hard. Forty years ago Dad, his two brothers and one of his sisters left for a new life in South Africa. When prospects improved for the remaining sisters, they married and moved out too. So that was the end of that era.

We travel on a double decker bus to see my Aunt Hetty, one of the twins, and I listen to the conversations around me. There seem to be a lot of new refugees in London now; Germans, Czechoslovakians, Austrians. Some are educated and speak quite good English. With my hard won Afrikaans I can understand those that do not and get the gist

4

of it. They are talking about Germany's invasion of Czechoslovakia, Poland's fears. About fleeing to England.

But the English on the bus are talking about everyday things. The price of bread, the latest fashion, film stars, work, home. Until war is declared they are hoping for the best. Then I overhear two women discussing whether their children will be evacuated or not. They don't want them to be. *They* are not making plans to move out of London lock, stock and barrel.

Hetty lives in Dalston and we travel to it through tree lined streets and Victorian houses. All of them at least double storey, some semi-detached, others terraced. We glimpse workmen digging in gardens all along the way. Even in Hetty's back garden an Anderson shelter is being sunk into the ground to give them protection during air raid attacks. Merely two curved sheets of corrugated iron bolted together.

However, it doesn't seem the design is that well thought out to me. Where will the water go when it rains. I suggest to Hetty that they put gutters in to take the water away from the roof. But she says that they have to cover the roof with soil. I don't mention that there will still be a problem with water, if it has nowhere to go. Look at the water filled trenches in the parks. 'With luck there won't be any bombs dropped on this part of London', says Hetty.

Nevertheless, she already has her pantry stocked with packets of sugar and rice, tins of corned beef and peaches, in case of shortages. After taking all this in my mother says she is going to look for an apartment a bit further out. Somewhere a little more leafy, is how she puts it. Somewhere with a nice dry basement for shelter. Once we know where I will be studying.

Hetty tells us that Rhoda, her twin, is still living in North London on the Finchley Road. She and her husband are in the silk business but that they are only recently back from a buying trip to New York. She asks if we would like to see Aunt Lizzie instead. 'No, we shan't see Lizzie', says my mother, in a resigned voice. 'She doesn't want anything to do with me now. Not now Phil has gone and her gravy train with him.' She is all pursed lips on the bus back to the hotel and when we get there immediately spends Phil's gravy on the best theatre tickets available and - back on fighting form - follows that with a slap-up dinner for us.

Lying in my hotel bed, hearing a taxi cab hailed and the burst of music as a club door opens - the noises of busy London nightlife right outside my window - I try to forget all the wonderful dreams I have nurtured of living and studying here. Try to concentrate on making my mind blank so sleep will come. Tonight that is how the future looks - an unknown blank. Where I will go and what I will do shall have to wait till the morning. But it seems a very long time away.

Postcard of MV *Dunvegen* Castle

2. Oxford University: August 1939

Hertford College, Oxford

It is, after all, to be Oxford for me and I am accepted for Hertford College. The College has long been known for its ability to produce good mathematicians and physicists. Before I leave London my mother does what she does best: shop. She can't get at our trunks so we buy pairs of bed sheets and bath towels which we have been asked to supply. I also get another pair of grey flannels (along with new braces) and a tweed sports jacket. Some woollen vests and two pullovers complete the list. I am ready for a cold English winter.

Everything fits neatly into a small cabin trunk that will go in the guards van but I pack some books and my essentials in my small, but heavy, leather suitcase which I keep with me. 'Just in case'. My mother insists on coming too so off we go to Paddington by taxi cab. The porter looks after us as if we are royalty and gets us window seats. It must be the stickers on my trunk – Durban, Port Said, Cairo, Rome, Gibraltar –

exotic adverts. The train has several stops en route to Oxford and we get a true feel of leaving a city and finding the real England. The green fields and trees remind me of home and I decide I will like being out of the city.

It is my turn to insist, so my mother grudgingly goes straight to the Randolf where she has booked a room for the night. I want to find my own way to Hertford College. Leaving my trunk with her I walk through Oxford, lugging my suitcase, wondering at the architecture. It is so unlike London. It's smaller, obviously, much quieter and - instead of buses and lots of pedestrians - bicycles seem to be the main form of transport.

Imagining I will have to find my way with the use of my small guide book, it is soon clear that it won't be needed as I only have to follow Broad Street until turning right into Catte Street. There, after no time at all, is the College. When I see the handsome entrance door, all deeply carved set in the stone façade, I feel insignificant but, strangely, at the same time very big. Proud perhaps - or awed - to have come this far.

Introducing myself at the Porter's Lodge I am delighted when a chap in a clean white jacket comes and introduces himself as my Scout. With relief, I hand over my suitcase which must have lengthened my arms a couple of inches. He shows me to a room in the Old Quad which is to be mine for my first year. I will have to move into digs for my second. It seems that most of the Colleges have been taken over by military departments. In Hertford it is Post Office workers that have been given rooms so there are only six suites for students left.

So many people and so few beds. It will have to be a room-mate instead of a suite for me. As I'm here first I bag the bedroom, my room-mate will get the sitting room. It does mean I'll be able to study without being disturbed. Pity, it would have been nice to have a sitting room. The rooms are not palatial. Everything in the sitting room is brown: brown furniture, brown carpet (what there is of it) brown curtains and even the cream paintwork seems to be turning brown. In the bedroom the iron bedstead is a bit narrow and the rug on the linoleum covered floor very small but I expect I will get used to it. There is also a desk and a chair, so there are the basics. My mother comes to inspect. The whole building is handsome and relatively new compared with much of Oxford although a few parts of it date back to about 1200. However, it gives the impression of all being ancient and she is very taken with the spiral stonework on the staircase and the bridge over New College Lane. Arched with handsome windows and bits of stonework, the locals call it Oxford's Bridge of Sighs, like the one in Venice. The Radcliffe Camera is very close to Hertford. Not only is it older than Hertford but it is considered an architectural masterpiece which certainly adds to the gravitas of the college surroundings.

The college library makes quite an impression on my mother too. I know because she doesn't say anything when we walk around, simply nods a lot. I like the quad with its plants on the walls and its grass. It's a garden right outside my door. We are both impressed with the Chapel; my mother always appreciates beauty and quality and the stained glass window inside it is both. Although I'm not religious I like it too and decide it will be a good place to do some thinking. Still and quiet - an oasis of calm - with no-one to disturb the process.

Within days I find there are a couple of real drawbacks to my bedroom. The New College clock is the first. It's in the bell tower up road and the ruddy thing chimes every half hour, all through the night. Next, is the street lamp. It's right outside my window and keeps me awake. I moan – they are a nuisance - but I know that I shall stick to my choice.

Finally my room-mate arrives. Hugh James Spencer-Palmer by name. A Rhodes Scholar straight from school in Nairobi. Fortunately, he seems quite happy with the room arrangement. We each have a washstand with pitcher and bowl and a chamber pot to pee in. Our Scout, Brown, (yes, to match the decorations) brings us a cup of tea at seven, followed by a nice lot of steaming hot water to shave with.

It's certainly very civilized here all except for the bathing. We don't have any bathrooms in our Quad. If Spencer-Palmer or I want a bath we have to go up some stairs, over the Hertford Bridge above New College Lane - at least it's covered with a roof so we don't get wet - and into New Quad. Then we traipse downstairs to use the bathrooms in the basement, carting our kit (towel, soap, wash bag and so on) with us. It's an arrangement out of the ark. When Brown comes in to see if I have everything I need I tell him this. 'What do they need baths for?' he replies, 'The young men are only up here for eight weeks!' After getting dressed we make straight for Hall to have breakfast. This is usually porridge and milk, sausage and black pudding, the occasional egg with toast and marmalade. Cups of tea of course. It sets one up for the day, a good breakfast.

A chap called Mintoff has arrived. From Malta. He's reading engineering — at least that's what I think he said but I don't retain the fact because I get such a pang of envy when he tells me he has a Rhodes Scholarship too. I'm surrounded by them. He's sharing rooms with another Commonwealth chap. But he doesn't look like the sort of man who'll go far, not as tall as me and, as my mother would say, rather scruffy. What a waste of a scholarship, I tell myself meanly but I am merely peeved and soon decide not to waste my energy on such negative feelings.

Mintoff (Dominic's his first name but he calls himself Dom) is a bit of a lefty. You can always find him by following the smell of his pipe. He and I take a few turns around town and I show him what I've found out. At first we go to the tiny Turf, our local tavern, where we manage to squeeze ourselves to the bar. We drink a couple of halves of beer (which I reckon has been watered down) and play a game of shove-halfpenny before we give up and go back to our solitary rooms.

Next, we try our hand at darts in the Kings Arms where there is a bit more room. Then it's the Lamb and Flag. This is the place for us as we meet up with all the Commonwealth chaps here who have signed up for the Airforce. And where there are servicemen pretty girls deign to tread. Both Mintoff and I soon have our eyes on one.

His pipe has grown on me so I've decided to give one a try. I did have a go at smoking cigarettes on the ship because I have Dad's silver cigarette case but I didn't actually enjoy it. I keep it stocked, though, because it's nice to whip it out and offer a cigarette to a girl. Pipes come in all shapes and sizes but I go for a simple straight number. I get a nice leather tobacco pouch and practice filling the bowl of it so I don't sprinkle the tobacco all over the floor. When it's filled and tamped down it can be a bit of a fiddle lighting. But the aroma, is pleasant. I save it for when I have a game of chess in the pub. Aids concentration. Gives me something to chew on.

Talking of which, dinner in College is not too bad. Hall is large and rows of long tables run up towards High Table where the Dons sit. The portraits on the walls and the dim shaded lights give it a very medieval feel. We scholars sit on wooden benches made shiny through bottoms buffing them over the centuries. And eat off the dark wood tables made shiny by the elbow grease of the cleaners over the centuries. Gowns have to be worn for dinner and we are served by the Scouts in their starched white jackets. There is a feeling of cloistered privilege here that I can't help contrasting with my forays into Soho or trips to the pub. They are two different worlds. West One and East End again. But I have to say I find I can fit into both. I like each of them, for their different reasons. In spite of rationing there are three courses at dinner. Usually soup, fish or meat, then pudding. It's alright but not special, there is never anything unusual on the menu. I mean boiled beef and carrots is hardly an inspiring meal. A bit of my mother's curry on the menu could really spice things up. But we do usually get ourselves a tankard of beer to help swill it down and good lively conversation and humour all help make dinner a pleasant time.

As I sit and chat and take in all the history of the place - soaking up the atmosphere - I thank goodness that I was not tempted by the offers I had to study in South Africa. Instead of sitting here surrounded by the beautiful historic architecture of Oxford I may have ended up surrounded by the heavy industry of Leeds.

3. Master of Science: South Africa, 1938-1939

Graduation Class Natal University College, Maritzburg, 1939
Eric, standing, third row, third from right

I had been working like stink to get my degree in record time. But in December 1938 I passed the examination for the MSc in Chemistry which was a tremendous relief. Professor Denison, my Physics and Chemistry Professor, was still encouraging me to go for a PhD. He knew I had not got the Rhodes Scholarship I had wanted so much — which also dashed his hope I would continue his research - so he had been making enquiries on my behalf. Right before Christmas I got a letter from him to say that Professor Barker, Head of the Chemistry Department at Rhodes University College in Grahamstown, was willing to offer me a scholarship of £210 per annum for chemical research in the Research Department of Leather Chemistry. Yes, Leather Chemistry, who could imagine such a thing.

He said Professor Barker was also offering me an assistantship at £240 per annum if I did not want the PhD offer. He said that PhD research at RUC was the route that a chap called Shuttleworth took. Apparently he went on to win the Proctor Research Fellowship at the University of Leeds against world competition. Leeds? I had never heard of the university there. It turned out that Leeds was Denison's *alma mater*. He thought that my PhD could also lead to a good career in tanning because he suggested that I could afterwards go to the Proctor Leather Research Labs in Leeds. But tanning! All I could think of were my mother's handbags and my father's shoes.

Denison strongly recommended acceptance of the PhD offer at RUC and wanted me to write back to him urgently. I knew it was a good offer and it was certainly kind of him to pursue it. But Rhodes University College, Grahamstown, was not King's College, London. And Leather, Hides and Skins Research — which was what he was suggesting now - was not *Some Observation of Dilute Gases*. I realised that I would have to do it of course but actually I did not want leather and I did not want Leeds.

Over dinner one night in the holidays I told my mother that as I could not get a scholarship to study in England I would obviously have to take the post in Grahamstown. I had been wrestling with the decision since the end of term and it was getting me down. She said nothing. I knew there was no way out and went up to bed with a heavier heart than usual.

The next morning, at breakfast, she said, 'Eric, I've decided. You've set your heart on taking your doctorate in England. We'll sell up here and go to London and you'll do it'. I was thoroughly taken aback, 'Sell the house?' She had built it. It was her pride and joy. I had expected her to live in it forever. 'Yes', said Mom, 'We'll sell everything and go to England. It's a pity about the timing but there it is. With The Munich

Agreement and the uncertainty about a recession prices have come down, which is annoying, but it cannot be helped'.

I was shocked. My mother would do that? 'But it means you will have to fund me', I managed to get out. 'Yes, you can pay me back' she replied immediately. 'Alright', I said, without hesitation. Without even thinking about it. I was over the moon. And so relieved. 'Thank you, Mom, this is wonderful. Just wonderful.' Hearing about our intended trip, Uncle Albert and Aunt Esther invited me to visit them in Jo'burg but I declined. They were always nice to me but had totally cut my mother since Dad died. 'They blame me for Philip marrying out of the faith,' said Mom, 'they never approved of me'. I pointed out that it was Dad who chased after her but she said, 'That's not the point in their eyes'.

Writing to Denison I explained that I did not want to make a life out of leather. I wanted to study in England but expected that I was on a hiding to nothing (I thought better of putting it like that as not everyone appreciated my puns). Perhaps King's College would not want me. But it was Denison who had awarded me the Lucas Prize for Practical Chemistry in 1937 and his faith in me seemed to be unshaken. It was very good of him to devote the time because he was Principal of Pietermaritzburg campus by then.

In March he wrote to the Dean of the Faculty of Science at King's College, London. He gave me a copy of the letter. He told them about my qualifications and that although the results of my MSc were not yet published he stated that I was Class I. I handed my thesis in and he said there was no doubt that it would be accepted. I would receive a degree of Master of Science at the graduation ceremony in May.

He also wrote that the MSc in our University demanded a sound, fundamental knowledge of inorganic, organic and physical chemistry, both theoretical and practical, as well as a compulsory dissertation or thesis. He told them that my thesis was a difficult experimental study of the *Kinetics of the Oxidation of the Nitro-phenols* (his subject). And he said that my character was excellent (I smiled at this bit, he had obviously never seen me out on a Saturday night) and he could 'recommend me without reserve as one worthy of being received at King's College and given senior status'.

I showed the letter to my mother and she nodded and said, 'Quite right too. I shall have to get a new outfit for the ceremony'. Sometimes I wished that she could just praise me a bit more and think of her wardrobe a bit less but after her generosity I could not fault her on support. Nevertheless, I missed Dad's enthusiasm and undisguised pleasure in my achievements. I kept Denison's letter and, many times afterwards, looked at it whenever I needed a bit of encouragement.

But there was trouble abroad. In January 1939 Hitler had threatened the "annihilation of the Jewish race in Europe" if war came. We hoped there would be no war and we could not believe such a terrible thing could result. Then in March he took all of Czechoslovakia and threatened to take Lithuania and Romania too. The Munich Agreement was well and truly dead. It looked like a world war was on the cards after all but we did not think for one moment his earlier threats would come to pass.

In the meantime I got a first class in physics and first class in chemistry and gladly attended my graduation on 20th of May. What a milestone. I was the proud owner of a certificate that I kept it propped up on my dressing chest until it sagged, which stated:

University of South Africa
Degree of Master of Science, E.A. Alexander
Natal University College of Science
Department of Chemistry (Physical Chemistry) 1938 Class 1

Although she would never say so to me, I think that Mom was proud of my achievement because she wanted to put a notice in the newspaper. I was ordered to go down to Leffler Studios in town and have my photograph taken. She planned to have it framed to put on the piano next to my other graduation ones. When I asked if a photograph was really necessary, she said it would be useful for our journey. Blackmail, but what can one do. She made me promise to have a haircut first, which I did, but I sneaked out wearing a jazzy tie that I hoped gave an impression of me that was not too staid. When the photograph was ready for collection I thought that I would look quite a mature twenty-three year old. Unfortunately, I actually looked like a naive schoolboy boy of seventeen.

It was time I earned my keep. I had already done some vacation research for Analytical Chemical Laboratories and Dunlop Rubber Company near Howick Falls where I was involved in testing the physical and chemical properties of synthetic rubbers. This was useful practical experience and was, eventually, to stand me in very good stead in wartime and post-war research. Offered a local job with the Anglo-Dutch firm Lever Brothers I was employed to do some oils and fats research. So it seemed that all those botany tests I had waded through would come in useful after all. The hydrogenation process had been discovered before the Great War.

After the war manufacturers like Unilever were turning vegetable oils into fats like margarine. With the Great Depression that followed the war butter came down in price which meant that the margarines and other manufactured fats were not quite such good value. So in the lab we researched new products involving processing a wider range of polyunsaturated fats. The company hoped that these fats could be produced more cheaply than butter. If they could also be spread more easily that was also be of great benefit. By processing the polyunsaturated fats successfully they did become soft enough to spread. Although I did note that by doing so the polyunsaturated fats became saturated once more. No-one was interested in this fact and we carried on with developing the product.

Whilst I was working my mother started to make preparations for our journey to England. She had decided to keep the tennis court next to our house with the idea, I think, of building another house when we returned. But there were the cars to dispose of. Mom thought she would leave one to our chauffeur, Bordon, and the other to our solicitor, Major Crawley. The silver flatware, bowls and tea set bought in London at Garrard would come with us and so would the embroidered table linen from Madeira. Of course she would never part with those. We had bought the silver when my father gave his business a try in London in 1926. It didn't work out but they had fun trying and visiting Europe.

Mrs. Alexander and friends, South Africa 1939

Everything else we owned she planned to auction off but she told everyone we spoke to that she was expecting depressed prices. I wonder now if that was to encourage them to attend. And she hoped that whomever bought the house might well bid for the larger pieces of furniture – those bought especially for it. Obviously the billiard table would have to one of them. It was a ship in a bottle, so to speak. The house roof had been taken off to get it in so there was absolutely no way we could ever get it out.

4. Air Raid Patrol: Oxford, September – December 1939

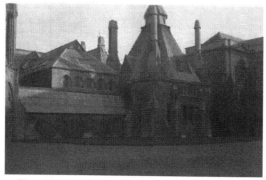

The Abbots Kitchen, Clarendon Laboratory

War. It was only a matter of time. The German army invades Poland and on the 3rd of September the Prime Minister, Mr Chamberlain, comes on the wireless to broadcast the news. 'This Is London', it starts, which reminds me of the first crystal radio set I heard in 1923. He explains that Germany will not retreat and so Britain and France have no option but to declare war with Germany. Then two weeks later the Soviet Union (they have a secret agreement with Germany) invades Poland from the east. So that is curtains for Poland. It is crushed between the two armies. Ten days later Warsaw has to capitulate to Germany. The newspapers are full of it.

Meanwhile, here in Oxford, all is quiet. The cinemas have closed and blackout is being firmly observed. One chink of light and a plane could spot it. The benefit for me of the plywood shutters is that there is no ruddy streetlamp shining onto my bed anymore. As I was up rather early, and no-one else was here, in a burst of patriotism I joined the ARP - the Air Raid Patrol - as a part time warden. I had to turn up for training. A Gas Course, then First Aid and how to use a stirrup pump, but all a bit basic.

When I'm on duty – three nights a week - I put on my black gumboots, my armband and black steel helmet and make for the warden's post. Because the whole thing is all a bit new here, our post is actually in the kitchen of a large detached house. Whilst we volunteers wait for the call to action we sit drinking cups of tea and playing cards or chess to while away the time. I can just see my mother putting up with that in her house. I like to tell them a different joke every time I'm on duty so I make sure I have one ready. If I can get them laughing it makes the evening go a bit quicker.

If the air raid siren goes we put on our tin hats and patrol the streets, encouraging people to 'Take Cover' in case any bombs fall. Mostly that means their getting into the cleared out coal cellar or the cubby hole under the stairs but it may be they have to go to the public shelter. Either way they need reminding to turn off their gas at the mains, open their windows and fetch their gas mask. We have to patrol like that all night if necessary, seeing if anyone needs help, reporting water leaks or breaches of blackout. The bigger the houses the worse they are at this basic precaution. But nobody takes very kindly to blackout enforcement and I decide its best not to respond to rude comments from angry householders.

When a siren goes on evenings I am not on duty I still put on the tin hat and my overcoat and take straight to the streets. But we're not allowed torches and I've tripped over a few kerbs not to mention bumping into a several lamp posts so I've taken to walking down the middle of the road. On several occasions I've nearly been mown down by bicycles that are silently making their way down the middle of the road too because they are not allowed lights.

It is definitely not the most comfortable job. We often have to cart a stirrup pump with us in case a fire breaks out (it never does) and we don't have access to any lavatories (a real inconvenience). So far I have had to pee behind trees, in the churchyard and sometimes behind buildings. There are several hedges I feel totally responsible for keeping well-watered.

My mother tells me that she is keeping busy by helping Hetty improve on her blackout arrangements. Apparently, their system of using paper tacked to wooden frames that had to be put up every night was quite unsatisfactory. Now she and Hetty are sewing some curtains made out of the heavy sateen material that's on sale especially for blackout. They will only have them downstairs and the family are going to bed in the dark and undressing on the landing using candles as it has no windows. If they are having that much trouble in one small house I can imagine what a headache it must be trying to stop electric light seeping out from buildings with large windows like factories and churches, or shops and hotels. Blackout is a real bugbear. It takes so long to do and the lack of light gets everyone down. My mother says she is not going out at night because of the hazards. She is afraid she will fall down and break a bone or get run over by a motor car that's driving without headlights.

At first being on ARP patrol was exciting. I felt quite important. Doing my bit, sort of thing. But as the planes have yet to drop a real bomb on Oxford there's been surprising little drama. Making sure everyone is safely under cover when flares are dropped is about the strength of it so far. By now everybody is given a war job. Even college people are fire fighters, air raid wardens and so on. I see undergraduates practising in their quads but I don't find it exciting any more. In fact I feel a bit of a fraud. I only do it now because it has to be done.

In October, only a month after war is declared, the British naval battleship *Royal Oak*, anchored in the deep water of Scapa Flow, is sunk by a German U-boat with 800 men aboard. To add insult to injury the submarine escapes undetected. It was thought that the anchorage in the Orkney Islands was impregnable. Everybody is shocked.

When I think about it these sinkings (drownings) and bombings (deaths) I feel oddly detached, like it's all a big story out there, happening in another world, in another time zone. Quite surreal. Then, every now and then, I am reminded that it's very real when more women with their babies and toddlers arrive, evacuated from London, or the sky lights up in the distance, possibly their very homes being bombed. Paperwork is our latest national weapon. A National Registration Census is taken and we have all been issued with an Identity Card. It has ones name and address on it and my Registration Identity Number is BACE 2. Soon we will have ration books too. When we do it may change my opinion that dining here in Hall is quite good. Very important dining. Fuel for the brain. Rationing is not something that comes easily to South Africans, we're used to quantity as well as quality. Since November bacon and butter have been rationed so now it's down to bacon twice a week, an egg a week and only the luxury of a kipper or couple of kidneys now and then to break the monotony.

In December, three British cruisers (*Exeter, Achilles* and *Ajax*) engage the German pocket battleship, *Graf Spee*, in the Battle of the River Plate. The *Graf Spee* has been attacking merchant ships that Britain relies on for supplies: food and coal, that sort of thing. It docked in Montevideo for repairs but when it had to leave port the British cruisers convinced the Captain that it was up against such strong opposition that he scuttled his ship. Everybody is delighted. The score has been evened.

Whilst all of this is going on I'm still tucked away in quiet Oxford, studying the supersonic dispersion of gases. I do know how lucky I am. In case we are actually bombed, I take some snaps of the University Museum - the old Clarendon Laboratory and that part of it called the Abbott's Kitchen - for posterity. I kept my old Brownie ticking over for years with glue and tape (out of sentimentality not need) but it finally had its day.

On gaining my first degree my mother bought me a Kodak Six 16 folding camera which came into its own when we were on our way to

England. Photography is quite a big thing here now and colour photography is the latest. There's a room devoted to the art in the Clarendon Lab and several talks and demonstrations. I have attended a few and will invest in a more sophisticated camera when I am finally earning. It is a science, photography, as much as an art.

I also attend the odd lecture if I think it will be useful or interesting. For example, Solly Zuckerman is giving a lecture and I go along to that. For a variety of reasons. He was born in Cape Town, of immigrant parents and studied anatomy and zoology. He also published a book, *The Social Life of Monkeys and Apes,* and I have always been fond of monkeys since having one as a boyhood pet. Now Zuckerman teaches here, at Oxford, and takes an interest in the ARP. With all these parallels, along I go to see what he's like. Quite obviously brainy but not dull. He comes across as a bright spark, a human dynamo. It is an interesting but not instructive interlude that makes a pleasant break in my solitary and intense research.

Similarly, I have joined some of the Science Societies in the belief it will help my studies. Having now attended a couple I realise that these are for people who are so passionate about their subject that is all they want to talk about. Therefore, NO Jokes. Nor do the meetings help ones degree but simply use up valuable studying time. There is a war on and no time to waste. Instead, I buckle down and work six days a week in the University Museum's Chemistry Laboratory housed in the Abbot's Kitchen. Abbot's Kitchen sounds odd, but it's called that because the octagonal Victorian Gothic style building is based on the Abbott's kitchen at Glastonbury.

As it is, it is the only place that has a ceiling high enough for my manometer which is eighteen feet tall. The Clarendon Laboratory next to the University Museum does have a lofty palm court sort of affair which was designed for tall apparatus but I don't think they thought of anything this tall. It's not high enough. And as the top floor is being used for other research the physicists involved are not keen that someone else might be in and out at any time of day. People always ask what I need a manometer for. It is getting very tiresome being asked the same question over and over again and having to go into long explanations so now I say, 'I need it to measure the pressure of the vibrating sources of change of velocity of sound in tautometric gases which are changing state'. They don't usually ask anything more after that.

5. Mother and Son:
December 1939 – July 1940

Mrs. Alexander and Eric

Christmas in London is a strange sensation. My mother has taken an apartment in Turnham Green. It is in a very smart block called St Catherine's Court which she has tried to make look festive. But without Dad Christmas has lost some of its sparkle. Also, Christmas in a cold climate is not all it's cracked up to be. Robins and snow on Christmas cards are all very well but on the ground it's a different story.

Nevertheless, my mother does her best and plans a tremendous meal. We ask Hetty and her family if they'd like to come and share it with us. My mother has been buttering up the butcher for weeks and (with additional monetary incentive) he has come up trumps or, rather, rumps. When they hear that we are to have a beautiful roast and all the trimmings they say, yes, immediately.

Whilst in the flat my days are spent sawing in my little bedroom at the back. I brought a pistol with me to England (Dad's old one that I used to keep under my pillow) but I never declared it. I reckoned I might need it here. But now I've heard that one must report weapons because it's wartime. It has worried me all Michaelmas term. I keep waiting for the hand on my shoulder and imagine myself marched off to the police station.

Fortunately, studying physics requires a certain amount of mechanical nous. It is often necessary to make or fix equipment and apparatus. It is all part of the invention and experimentation process. So I have skills that do come in handy for all sorts of things. Such as cutting up my pistol with a small hacksaw. Every day I put a piece of sawn-off pistol in my pocket and go for a walk alongside the river. When no-one is looking I drop it into the Thames. Of course I have to get rid of the bullets too. So I also put one of those into my other pocket every time I go out and drop that into the river too. Oh, what a tangled web we weave. By the end of the next holidays I should have disposed of all of it and in years to come they may find the remains and wonder what crime it conceals.

Back in Oxford I am chilled to the bone. February is bitter. It is the coldest winter I've ever known. In my room I work wrapped in a blanket, encased in the armchair right up close to my fire. I worry that Brown has forgotten the coal, or, more worrying still, cannot get any. It's been in short supply. How I miss the South African sun but, I have to admit, that's actually the extent of it. I enjoy being here in spite of the privations of war and the weather.

Although I am numbed to the core my research is going well. The labs are only a brisk five minute walk away so by the time I get there I'm warming up. Professor Hinshelwood himself (Professor of Physical and Organic Chemistry at Trinity) is taking an interest in my work. By great good fortune I had quoted one of his papers in an article in Transactions of the Faraday Society in South Africa in April 1939 (*Reactions of*

Metallic Salts and Complexes, and Organometallic Compounds) and it was reprinted in Great Britain in September and of course he read it.

I was nervous but thoroughly thrilled when he sent a note to ask me to come up and see him. Fortunately, when we meet in his office, we immediately hit it off. His major text is *The Kinetics of Chemical Change in Gaseous Systems* and my MSc was *The Kinetics of the Oxidation of the Nitro-phenols* so we are definitely on the same wavelength. But, generally, one day is much like another and the term passes by with little else of note.

I have been out with several girls now but it's not easy getting intimate. Girls are only allowed in college during the daytime which is when they are usually in lectures or working. In the evening most girls won't be seen dead in a pub without a man so I have never been lucky there. A few of us chaps from College usually go to the cinema at least once a week but if I do get chatting to a girl there is nowhere to go afterwards. Even if I do manage to throw off the other chaps. There is at least one dance every weekend but we have to be back in College by midnight which doesn't leave a lot of time for spooning.

My mother assures me - with a little hint of martyrdom - that she is coping alone. She sees Joyce, her friend from previous visits who lives in Golders Green, quite a bit. As my mother could not get her huge trunk up to her flat Joyce is storing it in her garage. The local Hippodrome there is one of the first to reopen which pleases them because they both love the theatre. She also goes to her friend, Margaret, in Greenwich where the cinemas are open again. When my mother worked in the Cape Town theatre she met and entertained many of the famous visiting stars and loves nothing better than to see them larger than life on the screen. When I go up to visit her in the spring I travel into the West End and find the night life there as busy as ever it was. The cinemas and theatres are packed.

I need to do something that doesn't involve my brain (too much concentration is frying it) so as I'm not sporty I take in the shows. It's my mother's influence I think. If I haven't much time I often pop into the

Windmill Theatre for a beer which I always enjoy. Nearly as much as the non-stop revue that runs from mid-morning till midnight. Apparently it's quite something to be a Windmill Girl. There's a chorus of dancers with lovely legs and group of girls with beautiful bodies.

The first bit is non-stop action as they tap their hearts out between the comedy acts. Then, in the second act, they come on naked but stand as still as statues. Because they are naked they are not allowed to move because if they do they are breaking the law. They can only take up dramatic poses in a themed tableau. I prefer the Paris version I saw with my parents at the *Folies-Bergere* in 1926 (although still a child they took me with them wherever they went) where the girls concealed their nudity with tiny costumes and props strategically adjusted with deft movements of the arms.

The Windmill Theatre is trying to outdo the cinemas but there are far too many of them for it to be a fair contest. Queues of keen cinema goers can be seen snaking right round the corners of the streets in the West End. I have never enjoyed the cinema on my own which is why I prefer to go for a drink where there is always someone to have a few jokes with. In the nearby dance halls and bars everyone is out to enjoy themselves too. Plenty of folk are pleased to take or make the most of the current situation. And the chaps in uniform are all too ready to link up with the prostitutes in Soho and seem willing enough to be taken advantage of with inflated prices in bars.

I notice too that the workers seem happier now that football and greyhound races are on again. Their women content because the children are around once more, all returned from their evacuation. The buses are also running alright and, apart from the fact that a great number of the shops are shut and many of the big houses are closed up, one would think there was no war. Except for the blackout. I must say that walking about London in the complete darkness was a nightmare at first. But I have practice on ARP duty and when you get used to areas of London it is really quite illuminating. I've bumped into more kissing couples and stumbled into more dark doorways with couples canoodling than I care to say. Everyone, especially in Oxford, is feeling that this war is all a bit of an anti-climax. The country has prepared so well that the Germans will not - people say cannot - bomb us. Then in early April, soon after Mr. Chamberlain tells everyone that the Germans are getting nowhere, they invade Norway, Greece and Yugoslavia. This is followed by the invasion of Holland and Belgium in May and, after the surrender of Belgium, the need for our British Expeditionary Forces to escape what could be the most terrible defeat.

All of us are fearful and then amazed when we learn that thousands of troops are being evacuated from the beaches of Dunkirk. Over four days they are rescued by not only the ships of the Royal Navy but also by hundreds of brave civilians who make it across the English Channel and back in every seaworthy boat - no matter how small, no matter how unsuitable – risking their lives to help our troops get home. 300,000 – that is the estimated number of men that needed to be transported back to Britain. The patriotism and bravery is inspirational and awe inspiring. But not all of them make it. The newspapers trumpet the nations pride and our pain.

By the time France collapses in June and Hitler sends troops in to Russia the mood is quite different. This is no phoney war. We all feel chilled. It does not bode well. Mr. Churchill gives a rousing speech about fighting and never surrendering and even more men enlist. In and around Oxford the fear of invasion is obvious as anti-invasion measures (roadblocks, the removal of road signs and names of shops and businesses that may identify a place to the enemy) are installed or instigated. But, when I visit my mother again in early July, I notice how everyone I meet in London is now united in purpose and defiant once more. All patriotically determined that the Germans won't get us although secretly fearful of just what might be in store. Food prices have gone up - and portions have gone down - but people with money (like my mother) seem to be able to get what they want within reason. Perhaps because of this - although she constantly tunes in the wireless for news of the forthcoming invasion like everyone else - my mother is uncowed until in late July a German raid catches Londoners off guard. Suddenly they are all taking to the shelters again.

I tell my mother that I've been accepted as a Member of the Association of Chemists. It was a good move to apply because the Air Ministry has offered me a Sciences and Engineering post. At £600 per annum. An unheard of large amount, apparently. 'That is a *very* good salary', she says gravely, giving me a very straight look. She means me to accept it. But I turn it down, much to her chagrin. I explain to the Ministry that I've come to study under my own steam and at my own expense and that I intend to get my D. Phil. I'll get that first, I tell them, then I can accept a post and be of more use to them. I can't be deflected now.

I will return to Oxford and work twice as hard and twice as fast. No summer vacation for me. The country might need every scientist it can get. I think of Dad and how proud he would have been to see me gain my doctorate and that to do so will enable me to fulfil my promise to look after my mother. But she only tuts, and shakes her head, and lets it be known generally that I have made the wrong decision. I can understand why but I won't change my mind.

6. Dad: South Africa, 1936

Phil Alexander

I was a bit strapped for cash in most of my second year at university. I would not ask my mother for any more. There was this Dutch chap, Pieter – older than most of us – with whom I was sharing a room to keep costs down. He was put up by the SAR Railways. They often sponsored fellows. However, he was struggling with the course, especially physics. He asked me if I could help. Said he would pay me.

He had the same lectures as me but mine were two weeks before his. So I said, 'Alright, I'll teach you what I learn for ten bob a week. I'll have a lecture on something, learn it, then two weeks later we'll go through my notes and I'll teach it to you'. So it helped me learn too and made some spare cash into the bargain.

Generally, it was more a case of explaining to him how things worked and ways to learn things. Coaching him. For example, ages before, when he was having trouble learning the reactions of elements in the Periodic Table he said to me, 'It's impossible, I'll never pass. There are 57 equations to learn and I can't do it'. I said, 'No, there are only nine basic equations depending on the position of the element in the Periodic Table. All the others are derived from them. If they ask you a question you can develop the answer from those nine'. I had to give him lots of examples but he finally twigged.

It was certainly a good way for me to earn spending money throughout the remaining years of my BSc. Dad would have approved of this display of business acumen — albeit by a rather late learner - although he would have preferred to fund me I know. I think of that awful second year at university often and the horrible feeling in my stomach when Bordon arrived unexpectedly to collect me from my digs and drive me home during the first term. I was expecting the worst when we reached the hospital in Durban.

Dad was lying in bed and said that his left side was numb. His speech was slurred. I was relieved because after what Bordon had told me about his collapsing I had imagined him paralyzed and unable to speak. I sat with him for an hour or so then he said, 'You had better go home and see your Mother. She will be wondering where you are'. I had to ask him to say it again. And I wondered how it was that a man who was so seriously ill was nevertheless still worried about someone who was not. I went home to Mom. I think she must have been in shock. She forgot to tell me off for my long hair and scruffy appearance and did not moan at me for going straight to the hospital. We had a very quiet supper. I was tired and worried, Mom was nervous and worried.

We visited Dad the next day. He was very sleepy and his speech was still slurred. Mom told him all about the staff, those who had rung from his office, who had called by. I told him all about my studies. But it is difficult thinking of things to say when it is not a two-way conversation. The next morning I studied at home and visited Dad in the afternoon. I went every day for ten days and some days Mom came with me. But

Dad did not seem to improve much which was worrying. Then the doctor said he could be nursed at home. There was nothing more they could do for him.

I helped Joseph and Bordon move his things into another room, got a commode and a table set up by the bed. Mom supervised. This involved her telling us to move everything several times. Mom contacted Auntie Rae and Uncle Albert. We only saw them on high days and holidays but suddenly they were on the telephone every day. They tried to tell Mom what to do. They had obviously forgotten that she is a force to be reckoned with.

I sat with Dad and studied whilst he slept. When awake he talked to me if Mom was not around. Either his speech was improving or I had got my ear in. Mostly he asked how I was doing and told me that he was very proud to have a son at university. How impressed he was with the way I had always applied myself and that he knew I would do well. He said how useful a good education is, that he never had one and had to use his wits instead. And he told me about the unusual things he had done in his life. Things I had heard before but was now pleased to hear again.

The next day it was his birthday. And it was Mom's birthday too. On the same day. No-one can get over the co-incidence whenever I mention it. Mom says that she thought Dad was spinning her a line when he told her he had the same birthday. Apparently she said, 'No, that's my birthday'. And he said, 'It must be fate. Now you will have to marry me'.

Usually Dad bought Mom some piece of jewellery for her birthday and Mom bought Dad something like a silk tie or a stick pin. Because he was ill in bed she bought him a pair of silk pyjamas. Dad said to me, 'Buy your mother carnations. Enough to fill the crystal vases. Like we did whenever we had a party'. So I bought six dozen - 36 red ones and 36 white - and put them in the vases on the sideboard for when she had breakfast like he asked. And I put one in a vase by his bed.

I don't think either Mom or Dad were in the mood for presents. Most of the presents I had given Mom over the years were kept in the bottom drawer of her dressing table anyway. And I used to give Dad cigars but he gave up smoking those. In the end I bought neither of them a present. Dad being so ill, and Mom being so odd, meant I could not think of anything suitable anyway. Instead I got them both the biggest birthday cards I could find. Dad's had a picture of a motor car and Mom's had flowers and lace. I told them that I would get something for both of them when Dad was better. Dad said, 'That will be splendid'. Mom did not say anything. Dad dozed a lot the next day and the day after that he became very melancholy. He told me how much he loved Mom. That she always was the only woman for him. That the death of Doris, my older sister, was a terrible blow. How he blamed Mom for quite a while but he realised that that was a destructive emotion. That they managed to muddle along. How finally I was born and they were both over the moon.

Then I was ill with meningitis, nearly died, and that after that Mom was obsessed with me. That she never paid him any attention which is why he strayed. Then he said, 'But because of you we didn't separate.' He smiled at me and I knew he meant 'because we both love you', not blaming me. Still, I felt almost guilty. I did not want to hear any more. I said, 'Yes, Dad. That's okay Dad. Sleep now. Rest'.

But he wanted to talk. Rather, he wanted to confess. That is what it felt like. I remember thinking, why can't he tell it to a friend like anyone else. But it was as if he had to get it out. He said that he was never unfaithful in Durban. Only when he was away on business. That it was because Mom had no time for him. I felt uncomfortable. I definitely did not want to hear. I tried shutting my ears and concentrated on looking like I was listening. I nodded a lot.

I wondered if this was what most fathers do when their sons grow up - share intimate experiences with them. It felt strange. Like I was his chum. In my experience chaps only boast to each other, never admit to failings or being afraid of anything. But Dad had always been so sure of himself. Or was he telling me because he thought that this might be his only opportunity to set the record straight.

He then talked about the time Mom tore all her new clothes up and, as I heard that, suddenly something made sense. The penny dropped. I remembered when she did it. I remembered how she did it. So, she had found out that he was sleeping with another woman. *That* was why she tore all the clothes up. Then he said how she never, never forgave him. Never slept with him again. And I wished that I had not started to listen. That I had put my fingers in my ears. I pretended to myself that I had not heard that last bit.

I remembered the other times she got mad with him, at the club, at parties, during racing weeks. And I could see Dad at those places. Always smiling, always laughing and joking. Dancing with everyone. Men would say, 'Your father is such a good sportsman'. But women would say, 'Phil is such a charmer'. Dad liked women. I could tell that as I got older. The way he listened to them, the way he made them laugh.

'But I have always loved your mother', I heard him say. I don't know what else I had missed but I saw a small tear run down his temple. So perhaps he told me because he wanted Mom to forgive him. Then, before it was too late. And I thought it was time I called the nurse. I said, 'You had better rest, Dad, you're still very weak'.

Then he grabbed my wrist with his good hand, with such a firm grasp. He was seriously ill but his grip was like a vice. Still, I remembered he had batted and boxed. 'Look after your mother, Son', he said. 'Look after your mother'. And I replied, 'Of course I will, Dad, of course I will'. And he let go of my wrist, and closed his eyes, exhausted.

When neither Mom nor I were there the nurse sat with him. And she stayed with him at night. She bathed him and helped him onto the commode in the morning. She and I took it in turns to shave him. I helped him eat, cutting up the brisket stew Mom cooked for him, or spoon feeding him the matzah ball soup she made. But as each day went by Dad got more anxious about our finances. Mostly he talked about Mom and how we would cope when he was not around to provide for us. He asked me to call his insurers and arrange for their agent to call.

The insurance broker came with a large black briefcase. He knew

Dad well. He obviously respected him and he said how sorry he was to see Dad indisposed. But neither Mom nor I were invited to be party to the conversation which did not last longer than ten minutes. 'Don't worry', the broker said to me when he left. He patted his case, 'You will be alright. Everything is taken care of''

But Dad soon became anxious again. He said that if he stayed like he was he would be no use to us. That he did not want to be a drain on their savings. That he had made a will, that the house was all paid for, that he had a good insurance policy. I told him not to worry. That he would get better. That I would get a job and provide for them. Then he took a turn for the worse. That evening I noticed his speech was slurred again. His movements more restricted.

He told me again that he was worried about Mom. That she would be much better off financially if he died. He asked me to get the nurse. He needed to sit on the commode. By this time it took both of us to get him onto it. He said he would be some time. I left him and the nurse to it. But I heard him tell her to leave him for a while. Much later the nurse came onto the landing, calling in panic. 'Mister Eric, come, please come now. It's Mr. Alexander. He's had a fall'.

BSc Graduation Natal University College, Pietermaritzburg 1938
Eric standing back row third from left

7. Digs & Dogfights:
Oxford, August – December 1940

The Old Clarendon Laboratory, Oxford

I manage to find some very good digs for my second year at Oxford. They are a nice family, my room is a good size, Mrs Bennett's cooking is more than acceptable and it is not too far to walk to South Parks. But the best bit about it is that I am out in the real world and not confined to barracks so girls are once more on the agenda. Barbara, who looks younger than me, is the landlady's daughter and she is friends with the lodger next door, Margot, who looks a bit older than me. She's a PT teacher from up north with the most beautiful flaming red hair.

Margot takes a shine to me so that when I ask if she'd like to come out for a coffee in town she says 'yes' right away. The next time we go out to the cinema and I buy her some Maltesers. She's likes them and is surprised that a student can run to chocolates and before I know it, it's a regular thing. Both the Ritz and the Electra cinemas are within easy walking distance. In between times I take her to dances where swing music is all the rage. It's so crowded I hope nobody notices that I'm no expert. She has come to the Lamb and Flag with me but much prefers to drink in an hotel, the Randolf preferably, but the Mitre is acceptable when I tell her visiting stars sometimes go there.

On a warm late summer weekend, when the Battle of Britain is at its height, Margot and I make for the countryside. We take the bus as far as we can go then hike up the hills. The whole Cotswold area is a positively romantic vision of old England and I like the soft golden stone of the houses. I can see why my Aunt Rhoda is so taken with it but it's the space and the greenness that I most enjoy, reminding me as they do of trips to the Drakensbergs at home. We lie on the grass and, after kissing and cuddling a bit, we listen to the gentle sounds of the birds and gaze at the clear, cloudless blue sky. Suddenly our peace is shattered.

First we hear a plane. Is it coming from London, going to Bristol? No, there's more than one. It is an enemy plane being chased by one of our fighters. We are well and truly taken by surprise when they start firing at each other. The sound is shattering: shells bursting, machine guns rattling, engines roaring. Margot and I can do nothing but lie there on the grass, frozen. Shielding our eyes from the sun, our free hands grip each other's tightly as we watch the most amazing unscheduled display. Horrified but at the same mesmerized. Then, as suddenly, they are gone to have their dangerous dog fight over to the north. When we can no longer hear them, all we see over the brow of the hill is a trail of smoke. We hope it's not the Spitfire and, subdued, we make our way back down the hill and head for home.

Since then the Germans have bombed Bristol and when they bomb London in early September I telephone my mother. She tells me she slept right through the first air raid siren. However, since then London's East End has suffered terribly from bombing. It's the docks and ports that the Germans are intent on smashing. My mother telephones me (which is an unusual event in itself) to tell me that when the Germans are bombing the docks the ground shakes and the sky is ablaze with fires. She was staying with Hetty when they had a particularly bad raid.

'Thank God', says my mother, 'that I was with family - of a sort - because it felt like my last night on this earth'. For a short while afterwards she refuses to venture out as she cannot bear the thought that she may have to use the 'inadequate' public shelters. One night, after attending the West End theatre, she was forced to take cover in the underground during an air raid warning. For a while the discomfort of it (she said the smell was the worst bit) put paid to her evening theatre outings until she decided on matinees only, on the basis that raids are mostly at night. Not much stops my mother enjoying herself.

Meanwhile my studies in Oxford are coming along but it's been an uphill battle to date and I have had to come up with some pretty ingenious solutions. Professor Hinshelwood is now guiding me in my research and the subject of my thesis has evolved. Having someone interested who understands the problems I have and can inspire me, makes all the difference. He's a nice chap. Quiet and modest. The discipline that Hertford has always been well known for is mathematics but slowly it also became known for physics. Hinshelwood, however, is keen to promote physical-chemistry at Oxford and because of this he is especially pleased to have a post-graduate student who *is* a physical chemist.

My mother still comes up to Oxford to visit me every few weeks. Fortunately, only for the day. I mean, what student wants his independence compromised. She likes to visit Elliston & Cavell's, the big department store, and so we usually have tea there in Fuller's Café on the first floor. It reminds me a bit of the tea rooms in the big stores of the Cape. White starched tablecloths, pots of tea, plates of small thinly cut sandwiches and very large, fat slices of cake. I usually try to get chatting with the waitress (who is very pretty) but she always ignores me. Probably sick of students trying to curry favour.

Back in Turnham Green, my mother says she hears the bombers come over every evening. She says the smell and the smoke are the worst of it and she is hardly getting a wink of sleep. I suggest Oxford, but she says, no, it wouldn't be fair on her friends or on Hetty and her family. At least she can be of help to *them*. Then a bomb goes through the roof of Joyce's garage where my mother's stuff is stored. A lump of mortar has left a huge dent in her large Louis Vuitton trunk. The one she bought in Paris all those years ago. She doesn't seem so worried now by the thought of being bombed herself but the damage to her trunk she has taken as an outright insult. She tells me she thinks she will move her stuff south of the river, where she has heard of a flat in Blackheath near her friend Margaret.

Safely installed in Oxford, I am thrilled to be able to work in the new Clarendon Laboratory – it is absolutely excellent. Although the old one in the University Museum was quite a place in its day by all accounts, it is a bit dark and gloomy and the rooms are a little on the small side. The new laboratory has much more space and light. The University was a bit worried when there was talk at first that it might be requisitioned as a military hospital but, fortunately, someone somewhere put the point that here is a brand new laboratory space with lots of modern high voltage equipment right in the heart of Oxford. Also that there are physics graduates on hand that have research experience in the fields of engineering, sound, X-ray crystallography and so on.

In addition, the lab is right next to the Electrical Laboratory that has spawned students well versed in wireless and electron physics research. As much of all this research is concerned with instrumentation and industrial problems in general, what could be more perfectly suited to war work. Somebody listened. Luckily for us all there are now lots of bods beavering away in the new Clarendon Labs with plenty of room still available for me to use, as well as the Abbot's Kitchen.

I work all hours to achieve as much as I can and the additional facilities are a real help. I am only too aware that I need my qualification if I am to be of use but I do try to get time off from my studies whenever I can so that I do not get too bogged down. Having a regular girlfriend helps but both being lodgers means that it is rather difficult to get together with any privacy. Finally, one weekend I book an hotel for the night and treat Margot to tea - the full works - at Fuller's. We follow that with a film and she agrees to spend the night with me. I have no wish to become a father just yet and am prepared. The packet of French letters I bought at the barbers has been safely in my wallet for a month. We laugh and make love and laugh some more and I hope that this is the first of many such nights.

When Bristol suffers another bombing raid in November I find it ironic that many of the books from King's College – which I was so upset not to be able to attend - that were moved there from London last year when the university was evacuated to avoid bomb damage, have been destroyed. At the beginning of December following the heavy raids that affected London in October and November and the raging Battle of the Atlantic – where the loss of ships, submarines and planes, not to mention hundreds of lives, have the whole country in constant agony and fear - I go down to London and feel duty bound to ask again if my mother would like to come up to Oxford.

On one hand I hope she says, no, on the other, I do feel responsible for her. In the end I leave it to her (as if anyone ever made my mother do anything she didn't want to do). She says that she feels more secure in Blackheath and turns down my suggestion. After Christmas is over, I think she may have changed her mind. No sooner have I returned to Oxford than there is the worst bombing raid on London to date. I am shocked by the news and appalled at the photographs in the newspapers but am relieved that my mother has survived unscathed. St Paul's Cathedral has not been lost in the inferno that engulfed the city, as it was feared, and that has done more to boost morale than anything.

However, I point out to my mother that, among much else, the Surrey Docks, Madame Tussauds, much of the East End, The Natural History Museum, St Katherine's Dock and John Lewis on Oxford Street have either been burned to the ground or severely damaged. Perhaps she really should come up to Oxford. 'No', she says, 'If it is safe enough for the King and Queen to stay in London, it is safe enough for me'.

8. Doctor E.A. Alexander: Oxford, January - July 1941

Postcard of the Oxford Summer Eights

My examination is going to be in early July. Since Christmas I have been keeping my nose to the grindstone. It has been work, work, work, in order that I will complete my thesis in time. Hinshelwood and I meet in his rooms at the new Clarendon Laboratory on a regular basis but sometimes he comes to the Abbott's Kitchen to see me in action. We have several conversations about where I go from here. When I've finally got my doctorate. I say, obviously I want to do something for the war effort, using my knowledge. He doesn't say anything specific but he appears to approve.

Encouraged, and wanting to plan my future, I go off to the recruiting office only to be told rather baldly that I cannot enlist. Something to do with my having a South African passport. I tell them that I am a British Citizen but it cuts no ice. I am nonplussed and rather disappointed until they say that with my scientific experience I should contact the Admiralty. At the first opportunity I mention this to Hinshelwood and he says not to do anything more as he already liaises with them and will make enquiries. It sounds hopeful so I agree to wait.

After this last winter, what with the snow and the cold and the blackout, I am desperate for some warmth and sunshine. But as the days lengthen and the evenings lighten I feel a lot better. So does everyone else it seems. Oxford at this time of year is a hive of activity. Rather, a den of drunken revelry. I take full advantage of the party atmosphere. The undergraduates have had their Leavers Balls cancelled but they still manage to dance all night, ending up drunk and falling over each other. We post graduates however take the experienced approach, dispense with the footwork and go straight to the tipsy stage.

However, at dawn we all end up in the same place. With a group of friends, and as many girls as we can (and there are more of them than ever filling the spaces the chaps have vacated going off to war), we bump into each other in our punts on the river Cherwell. I have been practising a bit of pole-ing on my Sunday afternoons off in an attempt to impress Margot with my dexterity. She, however, is less impressionable than I hoped and is more taken when some college eights – whom I point out should not be on this river - whiz past us in their boats.

My mother tells me that we don't know how lucky we are in Oxford. 'London this May is Hell', she says, 'the worst yet'. The Blitz on the capital is not letting up. I ask again if she wants to come to Oxford. 'No thank you', she says. She tells me she has become quite adept at getting down to the basement during night raids, knitting to hand. I don't think she wants to give up her social life.

London is still suffering from them. Time Bombs (incendiary bombs) are dropped. Many of the fires are worse than they should be. Fire fighters have used water to extinguish them instead of sand. They need people on the ground who understand substances. Then part of the House of Commons is destroyed which seems to be a stab at the very heart of democracy. As the raids on airfields continue we hear that more

Allied ships have been targeted by U-boats. The Royal Navy is fighting a losing battle.

Since talking to Hinshelwood letters are flying backwards and forwards. First he writes to me to say, 'See me without fail at once as I have some important news from the Admiralty'. He encloses two letters which he says will explain the situation. The first is from the Ministry of Labour and National Service at Westminster. They've made some enquiries at the Admiralty, who would like to interview me. The second is a letter I must take to introduce myself to a Mr. Brundrett, the man at the Scientific Research Department of the Admiralty.

I am feeling apprehensive and excited. Not sure which one is uppermost. Excited. Yes, definitely. Can't wait to get out there and get stuck in. Doing research that will actually achieve something. Hinshelwood says that there should be some of the best scientific minds in the country working at the Admiralty. All in an attempt to win the war.

It is necessary to have the suit cleaned my mother insisted I had made in London when we arrived. Wool, double breasted, pin stripe, charcoal grey. Fortunately I haven't put an ounce of weight on. If the interview is a washout then it won't have been wasted because it shall have to be cleaned for my graduation anyway. Unless there are bombs in London on the day I am interviewed. Then I shall have to pay for it to be cleaned all over again. One gets filthy up there merely passing a bomb site.

Postcard of a London bomb site

In an attempt to keep occupied on the days leading up to my interview I walk along the banks of the Isis – which is what we students call the Thames - finally following the Oxford boat races. The combination of fresh air, water and green countryside is calming. On 30th May, the day after they finish, I take the train up to London. Travelling on the bus as far as possible, I then walk the last bit down Lower Regent Street. Posters everywhere encourage one to walk which is usually fine with me but today there is my suit to keep clean and my shoes to stay shiny.

The interview is at Dorland House at 12 noon and I am in plenty of time. I can tell quite early on that Brundrett is interested because his ears prick up at the mention of the word supersonics (that's variations in sound speed). Then we discuss sound signalling and devices. Keen to impress, I mention that I have broad interests too, keeping up with such things as Blackett's cosmic ray physics work and with crystallography. But he quickly brings the conversation back round to sound detection techniques. With each aspect of this we discuss he becomes more thoughtful. He says he needs young scientists who can put their academic knowledge to practical use and, as an Oxford graduate, I may well fit the bill. I think of my pistol, and nod.

Suddenly he suggests a post and quite as suddenly I say that I'll do it. Just like that. Not a moment's hesitation. We shake hands and I am ushered out. I leave walking on air and celebrate with a watery beer in the first pub I come to. It is only when sitting on the train back to Oxford that I think of all the questions I should have asked. On the first of July I get a letter to say that the Lords Commissioners of the Admiralty have sanctioned my appointment as a 'Temporary Experimental Officer in the Admiralty Scientific and Technical Pools'. It seems that civilians are only offered temporary posts. What it all involves I am not quite sure but am, nevertheless, thrilled.

Apart from one thing. I am to receive a salary of £350 per annum, plus War Bonus as applicable. This degree better pay off in the future considering I was offered nearly double that a couple of years ago with no doctorate. The letter informs me that I'll be working in the first instance at His Majesty's Anti-Submarine Experimental Establishment in Fairlie. That's in Ayrshire, Scotland.

They want me there as soon as possible and ask me to inform the Commanding Officer when that will be. Immediately I write to the Establishment to say I can report for duty on the 14th and B.S. Smith, the Superintending Scientist, soon confirms that date is convenient. My status will be that of a civilian officer, and I will not be required to wear uniform. Unfortunately, official accommodation is not provided, but they do write that every effort will be made by the Billeting Officer to help me obtain suitable lodgings at a reasonable charge. When I tell Hinshelwood all this a few days later, and that I've offered to start in the middle of the month, he points out in his quiet way that I've been a bit premature.

'Good to see a fellow keen as mustard', he says, 'but you've been a bit quick off the mark'. It seems that my examinations will not be over. So I write again and Smith writes back by return saying, 'There is no objection to your postponing your arrival until the 21st instant in order to complete your examination'. He appears to take no notice of my bad planning but I feel a bit of a fool. Hinshelwood, however, is very good. He says he will furnish me with a letter of reference which may mean I will be considered capable of more challenging work.

At last the examination is over. Blood, sweat and tears have gone into this degree. Getting my thesis ('*The Excitation by Collision of The Intramolecular Vibrations of Acetaldehyde on the basis of Sound Dispersion Measurements*' to give its full title) typed up has tested my patience more than anything. I have had to practically sit over the woman who's doing it as she taps away. How I miss Ruth. It isn't the scientific terms that are causing the problem - she is used to those - she says it's because my writing is practically unreadable. I must admit, she could have a point there.

Very soon now it will be farewell Oxford and farewell Margot. She promises to write. I never do, write that is, so I promise to come down and see her. I'll miss her of course, but I can't stop thinking about where I'm going and what I'm going to find. My mother says she will stay put. Says she's used to London life now and has made some friends. I suspect these are mostly the people she plays Bridge with. I suppose I should be relieved it's not a return to her poker days and that large sums of money are not involved. She says that her needs are few and basic. Only her whisky (which she buys on the black market), her cigarettes (very hard to come by) and a bit of fruit (gold dust). They may be few but they are hardly basic essentials. Items such as these are all luxuries in wartime Britain.

Of course she comes up to Oxford for the ceremony, delighted because she is able to wear her outfit. My mother bought the suit especially for the occasion when I first came up. It's a very smart, black embroidered wool jacket and she has now bought a jaunty felt hat with a feathery flourish in London to go with it. I must say that did show an impressive confidence in my achieving my goal. I've not always been so sure of it myself. Especially when I found Kings had moved to Bristol. Although as it turns out Oxford has been a safer place to live and study in than either London or Bristol would have been. And none of this would be possible if she had not believed in me and been so bold.

Eric, Oxford graduation photograph, 1941

The list is printed for all to see: Dr. E.A. Alexander 1941, Doctor of Philosophy, University of Oxford, Hertford College and as I read it a tremendous sense of achievement overwhelms me. We graduates visit the Norman Taylor Studio in the High Street to have our official photographs taken for posterity and as I wait patiently to have mine taken I have time to mull over how I got here. Unable to read or write capably until I was nine years old, having to catch up and work harder at school than anyone else, putting up with the jibes from other pupils and the frustrations of trying and not achieving. Then the absolute relief of gaining my matric and the joy of going to university.

Remembering the sacrifice and hard work that has made it all worthwhile, I think of Dad and how he always supported and encouraged me. I so wish he was here. How proud he would be. And as I sit - my hands resting on my gown, my fingers feeling the soft surface of my mortar board - memories roll over me like waves and I feel again the excitement of that first year at university.

9. Batchelor of Science: South Africa, 1935

Postcard of Natal University College, Pietermaritzburg

I was leaving home. My own man at last. I remember thinking that. It was a big step, an exciting one. I could not wait to stand on my own two feet. Before university started in January, Mom and I drove up to Pietermaritzburg to find me some digs. She was very particular even though it was I who would be living there. We looked at two places and they were not up to Mom's standard. She said to the landladies, 'The house must be clean and there must be three good meals a day'. I wanted the ground to open up and swallow me whole. Then we found Mrs. Willis who brought us tea laid out on a starched white tray cloth and a plate of homemade shortbread. She passed the tests with flying colours and I had digs for the term. Thank goodness.

Dad drove me up to Maritzburg for term and I think he was as nervous and proud as I was. First we drove to the Natal University

College campus where I showed him the main building with the science labs. It was quite an imposing structure of red brick with a tall dome on the top, a clock tower and big windows. All symmetrical, very classical. Another equally impressive building housed the library close by. Dad thought it was all very special.

Students were already wandering about the campus. Open necked shirts and sports jackets, piles of books tucked under their arms. Girls and young men chatting in groups. I remember thinking, I am part of this now. Then we drove into town, ending up at my new digs. When all my kit was in my room we sat and had tea with Mrs. Willis and I remember there were freshly baked jam tarts.

She told Dad that she was hard of hearing and he moved around in his chair to face her. He found out that she was a widow (her husband died of TB) and that she had a nineteen year old daughter, Ruth, and a son, Tony, who was crazy about cricket. Dad said he would try and get him seats for the test match.

We had eaten every jam tart and Mrs. Willis brought out a large sponge cake which was very good. After tea was finished Dad said to me, 'Alright, Son'. But he did not get up to go. I said, 'You better be off, Dad. You want to get back in the light'. But he still did not move and I practically had to march him out to the car. When he was gone Mrs. Willis said, 'What a charming man your father is'. She smiled at me and offered me another slice of cake and I knew that I would be okay there.

Mrs. Willis called Pietermaritzburg, 'Sleepy Hollow' and it did not take me long to see why. It must have been the quietest town in Natal. There were some very large, fancy red brick buildings but hardly any shops and offices, no industry and not that many bars and restaurants. There was not much to tempt me from my studies. But the thought of being able to go where I wanted, when I wanted, was heady. I would not have to answer to Mom. I would not have to do any explaining. I felt liberated. And a bit at sea.

It's a strange place, weather wise, Pietermaritzburg. It gets very hot and windy. And when the hot wind blew there was nothing for it but to strip off in our rooms and work with nothing on. The trouble was that the wind brought the dust so the windows had to stay shut. Then I would stuff the ventilator in the wall with an old vest to keep the dust out.

If there had been more trees in Maritzburg it would have helped but there was very little in the way of vegetation. The land was obviously fertile because shrubs like azaleas and roses grew around the houses, all very colourful. And most gardens had fruit trees and vegetables. I appreciated all of these but found the birds the most interesting landscape factor. They came in great flocks. Enormous flocks. Starlings mostly. They roosted at night in great numbers in the trees in the park - to keep safe and warm — and when they all took to flight together in the daylight they produced the most amazing undulating patterns.

At university I was studying chemistry, physics and mathematics. Because I did not have to do English as my minor subject (thanks to my stunt) I opted for biology, which was taught as botany and zoology. In the morning there were lectures and in the afternoon practicals, or pracs as we came to call them. But this was every day. I soon realised that with so many science subjects there was no time left for anything else.

Our list of books was long and therefore expensive. The library was large and well stocked but I found borrowing not too satisfactory. I needed to study the texts for longer than most of my fellow students and so I went on down to Shuter & Shooter, the booksellers in town, and bought what they had in stock. My main subjects were not too much of a concern. I had by this time worked out my own methods of studying things and committing them to memory. It was mostly a matter of repetition. The work was hard but it was interesting. But botany and zoology were new territory and I soon found botany very boring.

For example, when we were studying Food for Living Things (which included carbohydrates, sugars, starches, proteins, fats, oils etc) the practical work consisted of making solutions for such things as glucose, testing for sucrose, cellulose and so on. I wondered if I was not applying myself enough so when we studied cell division and looked at living tissue I invested all my beer money on my own compound microscope so I could work on slides in my room. But the fact remained that the subject simply did not excite me. Zoology, however, was much more to my taste. At our pracs we had to do vivisection on a frog – frogs as representative of Vertebrate (backboned) type – to expose the beating heart, to track the vein to see if the blood was flowing down, the stomach cut open. One had to have a pretty strong stomach oneself to cut something open while it was still alive.

With other things we only had dissection. But even then they had to be dissected immediately they were killed and we had to do them thoroughly. We studied brain structure and bones. We learned their growing systems. But there was no way to stop things rotting in the heat. When the zoology pracs were finished we immediately immersed our specimens in a tank of formaldehyde or they rotted before our eyes in the heat. Unfortunately they had to be fished out quite often to study them further which was a bit messy.

Talking of fishing, we also studied crayfish, *Cambarus affinis*, as a representative Invertebrate type (which includes earthworms, crabs and lobsters). We had to know all its skeletal muscles, the ones that are in the claw. Their claws are actually feelers which have a series of communication chords, each one communicating with the next so that they can feel their way along the ocean bed. I studied every book on zoology including our text book, *Animal Biology* by Woodruff. I recall that they were a nightmare to remember.

I grappled with it for days and then I remembered how I memorized the coalitions of the Napoleonic Wars at school and I made up a mnemonic: 'Why Do Poor Crayfish Make Ice-cream'. A strange rhyme perhaps. Why Do (*dactylus*) Poor (*propodus*) Crayfish (*carpus*) Make (*merus*) Ice-cream (*ischium*). Sounds daft but it did the trick and worked every time. I remember it still.

When we started studying crayfish I reckoned that all that was required of crayfish in my life was to be served up cold on a plate or cooked straight from the sea on a braai. Our lecturers thought otherwise and I quickly came to see why. There is something so amazing about the way they communicate and the method by which they digest their food. The crayfish has two stomachs and these had to be dissected too. We cut them open and flushed out the cardiac stomach and saw the teeth that chop up the food before passing it to the next stomach. A much more wonderful and complicated creature than the average lover of Lobster Thermidor could ever imagine.

There were eight of us students at Mrs. Willis'. The others were a noisy bunch. Whenever they came in they put the wireless on the minute they were through the door. Mrs. Willis was not bothered because she was deaf but it played havoc with my studies. None of them were studying sciences so after lectures they had most afternoons off. They came in for lunch then went off to their sports. They were friendly and used to ask me along but I had pracs most afternoons.

The Willis Family, Pietermaritzburg 1936

And I also had to study most evenings when Ruth, who was studying shorthand and typing, would often help me to revise. I have never been one of those gifted chaps that can simply get by winging it. I needed to read something several times, then read it some more. Then I had to repeat everything I learned until it had stuck. But when it stuck, it stuck. Forever. But I soon came to see that my ideas were as good as anyone's. Sometimes even better. I noticed that first in pracs. And I was to notice it afresh when I finally joined the outside world, working on research I loved, stimulated by scientists with enquiring and creative minds, essential traits for ground-breaking ideas.

10. A Secret Establishment: Scotland, August 1941

Postcard of the village of Fairlie, Scotland

No-one would imagine that this is where the boffins of Britain are trying to work out how to stop the German U-boats sinking our fleet. It's only a tiny fishing village, Fairlie, opposite the Isle of Arran. The Anti-Submarine Experimental Establishment was based at the naval dockyard on the Isle of Portland, Dorset. When the war started the Admiralty realised the south coast of England was too vulnerable to bombing so moved everyone up here to the back of beyond.

They took over Fife's boat building yard as a discreet site for the establishment. Situated on the coastline it's a ramshackle collection of large and small buildings, warehouses and sheds. Most are corrugated iron or of timber construction with the odd solid structure. From afar they look much the same, I am sure, as when they were used for building their boats and yachts. But now they are offices, design and engineer workshops, laboratories and canteen. To the north of the boatyard, along the shore, is a row of fishermen's cottages behind which is the parish church to the east. It all looks so normal. In addition, both small family houses and all the grander ones surrounding the village have been requisitioned for staff. With the addition of the personnel I would not be surprised if the population of the place has quadrupled.

Naval scientists were sent up here from other establishments as well as from HMS *Osprey* at Portland, now itself situated in Dunoon. Added to them are civilians like myself, various university lecturers and professors, all of whom are either scientists, oceanographers, mathematicians or engineers. So it has become a real hothouse of men and women all working together against the clock to gain advantage over the enemy.

The Establishment is supervised by a naval captain, William-Powlett. I am introduced pretty much right away. He wastes no time briefing me. German U-boats are decimating the Allied merchant fleet, with loss of essential supplies, and sinking our battleships with enormous loss of life. Now they are hunting in wolf packs. There is only one way to stop the U-boats sinking our ships and that is to detect them before they do. But we have got to improve the detection rate and by so doing, the hit rate. Too many targets are being missed. I have been enlisted to add my scientific knowledge and creative ideas to the pot. All very rousing stuff.

B.S. Smith — the chap who wrote to me in Oxford — is the Chief Scientist but my immediate boss is the leading research scientist, a chap called Paul Vigoureux. Says he was working at the Admiralty Research Laboratories (ARL) in Teddington - on high frequency echo-sounding - but originally he's from Mauritius. Smallish chap, spectacles, little goatee beard. He walks around with bare feet which makes me think of my childhood. I never wore shoes unless I had to.

Perhaps because of this shared background, Vigoureux and I have an instant rapport. Plus he seems to have a good sense of humour which is essential when spending any length time with me. He explains that submarine detection requires accuracy but it is not being achieved at present. That getting the correct location information is essential. Apparently Asdic - anti-submarine detection devices - are the answer. The Asdic set on a ship transmits a short pulse of high frequency sound through the water. When this reflects off a large object in its beam, like a submarine, it is echoed back. Technically this is referred to as echo location and ranging, using high frequency sound waves, a system which has been around since before the Great War.

This echo (called a 'ping' because that's what it sounds like) can be detected as an electrical current by a piece of equipment on the ship called an electrochemical range recorder. This in turn produces a visual record of the sounds received by the Asdic set. It is the most important piece of equipment in our Asdic system without which submarine echoes cannot be recorded and U-boats cannot be tracked, hunted and killed by depth charge.

These devices all stem from what I have been studying for my thesis which involved such things as the study of the dispersion of sound at high frequencies, absorption of sound waves, vibrational energy, using oscillators and magnetostriction apparatus: I could go on but needless to say this is right up my street and the thought of putting my knowledge to real practical benefit is exciting.

The range recorder looks a bit like a typewriter in size and shape. It has an iridium-tipped stylus which records these echoes onto chemically treated paper that runs over a roller. Marks are made through the paper onto the roller whenever the electrical current passes through the stylus. The chemical in the paper (which could be potassium or even cadmium iodide) then reacts releasing free iodine whenever this happens. This iodine is then deposited on the paper like brown ink. The echoes therefore appear as small individual marks on the paper. When they are joined up by hand or eye a pattern emerges in the shape of a curve.

These curves indicate the position and speed of the object, in this case a submarine. The ship can then torpedo it or drop a depth charge. However, recently, the styli are not producing clear enough curves.

They are smudged and are therefore not showing accurate enough information. Apparently, Smith worked on acoustics at ARL and at Portland on experimental range recorders and submarine echo-detection years before this war. With him were Charlie Dering, the main designer, and Ian Morgan. All of them are up here now but both Dering and Morgan are more concerned with the basic mechanical design and modifications to the Asdic range recorder.

Anyway, none of them think that the problem with the smudged traces is actually due to anything mechanical like the stylus. The paper that has been used to date is no longer available and a new paper is being used. The chemical used to impregnate it — I suspect it is potassium-iodide and starch - may be at fault. So it seems that a scientist is required to investigate. Vigoureux asks me, as a physical chemist, to put all my efforts into finding out if it is the chemical used in the paper that is causing the curves to smudge.

There is no doubt that it is essential to achieve more accurate curves that give true readings. The bald fact of the matter is, that if the curve is distorted it doesn't matter how well-designed the recorder is or how well it is fitted in the ship. If the target is not accurately pinpointed, a depth charge is wasted and the U-boat gets away. However, I am a little crestfallen. This sort of project is for someone far less qualified than myself.

However, I take a deep breath; the war must be won and the feeling of urgency is palpable here. I have no time to settle in and explore but it's straight in at the deep end. I'm introduced to two scientists, Alex Stewart and George Hodsman, who will help me in my task. Fortunately they are younger than me so I don't feel uncomfortable being in charge. Next I meet Dering and Morgan, with whom I liaise to understand the working of the range recorder fully. Then Alex takes me to see how the Asdic recorders work on our mobile laboratory in the Largs Channel off Fairlie Pier.

The ship is an old requisitioned whale catcher, SS *Icewhale*. brought up here especially for experimental work. The range recorders are all fitted-up down below and I suspect it is not the most healthy place to spend any length of time. Alex says it's not too bad at this time of year but if it is blowing a gale it is not very pleasant down there. And when the boat pitches and tosses everyone's stomach does the same. The Largs channel is deep enough for submarines (one reason they chose Fairlie for the Experimental Establishment) so we are able to test our equipment on the real thing.

Alex sits there listening for pings from the Asdic and at least one person always assists him to record the results manually. The experimentation with differing chemicals and the strength of solutions is dogged trial and error and over the next weeks we often work well into the evening. George, acting as my assistant, in the lab, Alex testing on SS *Icewhale*. Then we usually go back to our billets and sleep like babies. I've been very lucky and managed to find a house in Fairlie, instead of further away in Largs. I am pleased as it avoids having to take a bumpy bus ride to and fro every day.

I am billeted in one half of a house known locally as The Red House with the owner, Mrs. Hutton. Spence MacKay and his young family have the other half. He's an engineer in charge of running the labs here. Nice chap. A crystallographer, Norman Astbury – a Cambridge man, one of the Portland scientists - and his family are in the house next door. The family live in total chaos and the kids run wild. Typical disorganized academic type. The state of the place drives their landlady wild but it's always a happy place to be. His wife never minds if I drop in. As we're not far from the Establishment we chaps all walk to work together.

There's a substantial lunch in the canteen at the Establishment so Mrs. Hutton doesn't have to cook me a large meal at night. I often have a sandwich and a beer on my way home. Norman - very sensibly - frequently joins me. His wife is a terrible cook. I've heard the stories of the burnt offerings and I've noticed the charred remains on the compost heap. Hard at work, we nearly always miss the six o'clock news on the wireless so we do like to get home before the nine o'clock news. It's a ritual for most of us.

Waiting for Big Ben to chime at the start of the news in Mrs. Hutton's cosy sitting room, with the log fire crackling and the standard lamp flickering, fills me with such a sense of being in it. In a place that might really make a difference. It's history unfolding by the day, by the hour even. I think we all feel it. What turn of events - victory or disaster - may we hear about that will change the course of the war and our work to defeat the enemy.

Photograph of the mobile laboratory, SS *Icewhale*

11. The Walls Have Ears: Scotland, September 1941

Snooker at the Fairlie Burn Officers' Mess
Vig., 2nd left, and Eric, 2nd right

I am now finding the work thoroughly repetitive and not what I was hoping for at all. However, I have received the letter of reference Hinshelwood promised. He suggested it might mean I am involved in more interesting work, I do hope so and take it to Vig. Hinshelwood has indeed been generous. He says he followed my work with interest. That I am 'a very competent physical chemist' and 'had many difficulties to overcome and surmounted them with great experimental skill'.

He also writes that I've 'gone into the theoretical aspects of my work very thoroughly and can be deemed capable of undertaking any sort of problem in physical chemistry with good prospects of success'. Signed by the man who is Dr Lee's Professor of Physical and Inorganic Chemistry at Oxford, that carries quite a lot of weight. I do so wish that

Dad could have read this letter. Vig says leave it with him. 'Well, Eric', says Vig, a few days later, 'your Oxford Professor has certainly given you a glowing reference and my colleagues and I think we're wasting your talents. We must use your skills more widely on oscillators'. At last, my probation time is ended. I have proved that I am capable and reliable but now my superiors also consider me to be potentially creative and inventive too.

So I am set to help the team improving the cathode ray oscilloscope for echo detection as an improvement on the electrochemical range recorder. The range recorder (the same one I've been working on) used for submarine echo-detection clarifies the incoming echoes allowing them to stand out from the background reverberation. This is the noise or echo created after an explosion. Reverberation confuses - or masks - the important incoming echo that the Asdic set picks up from a target.

However, a cathode ray oscilloscope can do better. It completely distinguishes between the different wave forms of echoes and reverberation. A cathode ray tube, or oscillator, generates an electron beam onto a phosphor screen – sometimes referred to as a Radar (Radio Detection and Ranging) screen - on which it is possible to visibly track, or record in real time, the echoes of the target more easily without the confusion. The echoes are located using a quartz oscillator and - as with the Asdic set - improvements and refinements are necessary for better performance and detection. So the oscillator is what I start work on. At last a widening of my horizons.

In complete contrast social life here is very limited. On Saturday nights we take the bus into Largs in search of female company. In the hotel bar those of us who are not accounted for try and nab the prettiest girls and ask them out to the cinema. It is even worse than England here, you will never find a single girl in a pub. In fact here in Scotland you won't even find a married one. There's usually a dance somewhere but then we have to compete with men in uniform whom the local girls always accept as partners. To our face they say they have a duty, behind our backs we know they simply can't resist a uniform.

Fortunately, we single chaps are often invited to the local Fairlie Burn Officers' Mess. It's a large country house a couple of miles up the road from here. When we get there we have a couple of glasses of beer and play billiards with the naval officers. The single officers are billeted at Fairlie Burn and most of them have a wonderful sense of fun. It must be borne out of being cooped up on a ship, having to laugh to get through sort of thing, and we get on tremendously well.

Getting home afterwards is difficult in the dark and can be a bit treacherous but we tie our white handkerchiefs around our arms so at least we can just about make out the chap in front. A couple of beers inside us helps. It's a saving grace that place but, all the same, I'm beginning to miss Margot and plan a trip south to see her. A girlfriend in Scotland would be more convenient and it would probably be easier to have one who works here at the Establishment but at the moment Margot is still my girl.

Whilst I work on the cathode ray oscilloscope I am also to work on Asdic sets used in ships. Piezoelectric quartz crystal oscillators are the most important basic component of Asdic. A crystal oscillator is a device to generate an electrical signal with a very reliable and precise frequency. One of the most important features of a quality quartz crystal is that it provides a constant and stable frequency output whatever its temperature. So whether it is put near the warmer surface water of the Mediterranean, or into the cold deep waters of the North Atlantic, it will be reliable.

Generally, in nature, sounds can have frequencies up to 50 K/cs. There are exceptions such as the high frequency signals for echo location used by dolphins that can emit and hear sounds as high as 100 K/cs. The middle aged human ear, however, can only normally hear frequencies up to 20 K/cs. Oscillators with different frequencies are used for various applications. Most Asdic sets operate on frequencies between 14 and 22 K/cs. How the crystals are cut, what size and shape, the type and position of the plates, how a bank of oscillators is designed and the number of them in the array are all taken into account.

To make a quartz crystal oscillator the crystals are cut with a diamond saw into very thin slices which are then sandwiched between two metal plates to make electrical connections. The frequency of the crystal is determined by its cut and size and the frequency of its oscillations is final. It cannot be changed. When a source of electricity is applied to the plates the crystal oscillates. Expands and contracts in layman's language. When the voltage is reversed the expansion and contraction is reversed. This is called the piezoelectric effect. An oscillating signal is maintained at its constant rate by taking a voltage signal from the crystal and amplifying it and then sending it back to the crystal. Transducers are the name the Americans give oscillators. We do not use the term but it is a correct definition - oscillators can be classed as transducers because they do convert energy of one kind into energy of another.

Before the war the Americans developed piezoelectric crystal transducers (but they didn't use the more stable, and expensive, quartz crystal) either for communications in such things as wireless sets, or for military purposes such as in bombers or tanks where, for example, electrical circuits are needed to fire armaments. But here in Britain, after the Great War, we concentrated on using oscillators for anti-submarine detection weapons which do require the best quality quartz crystal. It is these basic components that I shall be spending all my time perfecting, adapting or developing.

Time is of the essence regarding improving both Asdic sets and the cathode ray tube as so many of our ships have been lost that supplies are short. With rationing we are already having egg-less weeks and are down to 16 ounces of meat a week. I used to have a 12 ounce steak every day for breakfast back in South Africa. With as many bananas as I could eat. Now I've almost forgotten what a banana looks like.

Fortunately, Churchill has persuaded the U.S. to lend ships to our merchant fleet. They can mass produce them in America to our design and the ships - which are little more than large hulls welded together - will be able to carry tons of dry cargo at one time. Food, war supplies, raw materials and so on. They have been named Liberty Ships because we hope that they will help us win the war. Food is on a points system as it is but now that rationing has gone up yet again there is no tinned food either. That means salmon and sardines are off the menu and even the American meats, previously available, are nearly impossible to find.

Liberty Ships bringing in supplies will help the war effort but labour is also in short supply. In an attempt to get more hands on deck (literally) the House of Commons has recently passed the National Service Bill. There is going to be compulsory conscription of young unmarried women. We could do with a bit more help here at the Establishment so may be lucky. I don't think any of us single chaps would mind a few more girls about either. Needless to say, I have signed to say that I have read the Official Secrets Act. The Asdic and everything surrounding our work is Top Secret. At the Establishment the scientists, in fact everyone here, have all signed and I have had to accept that I will not be able to publish most of the research I do.

In addition, after only a month or two in Fairlie, I am aware that none of the scientists here ever indulges in careless talk. 'Careless Talk Costs Lives', is the slogan. There are Naval chaps around every corner and in every pub making sure that never a word about our work ever slips out and we take care that it doesn't. The success of the war could depend on it. Of course, the same applies to everyone who works here. The clerks, research assistants, lab technicians, designers and operators are just as wary about what they say and to whom. Security is top priority. We none of us ever discuss any of our work outside the Establishment and never mention a thing at our digs or to friends outside.

It makes me think of my own little secret wheeze. One that, had I not succeeded with, could have blighted my days at university and could possibly have prevented my gaining the qualifications I needed to get here today. So although I have not a moment of guilt about circumventing such a short-sighted policy I don't talk about it. 'The Walls Have Ears', as they say in the newspapers.

12. High School: South Africa, 1934

DHS 1934: Eric, *standing 3rd row, 3rd from right*

My last year at Durban High School. Only Reichman who was in IVD ended up with me in VIB. That was the only trouble with moving streams. Ones friends were left behind. Most of us in VIB did not wear blazers anymore. It was not compulsory so we wore ordinary serge suits. Except the boys who had sports colours. They had wide gold braid on their blazers and you could see from a long way off that they excelled at one sport or another. If I had been good at sport I would have been proud of my prowess too. Instead I wanted to be good in my academic subjects. I wanted to be able to get on.

At the end of that initial term I came first and was third in exams. Considering I was bottom of everything when I started at DHS I was pleased. Exams were always more difficult for me. In term time I could work hard and swot at weekends but during exams I hardly ever had time to finish. I did not have time to plan. Never had a chance to read things through. That was why I did not do so well in English. In other subjects I worked out that it was best to write the important points down first. So at least I got the marks for them. That method does not work with languages.

For the rest of the year in VIB I worked like mad. I badly wanted to go to university to study science. In our final term I came first in everything except languages. It was that blasted Afrikaans again. I came second overall and Lapin came first. He was good at languages as well as all the other subjects. I had spent as long as I could remember before I went to school copying over and over again, trying to keep my writing in between the lines, trying to make it neat and legible, trying to please my parents and my tutors. And since then I had spent all my school days slogging away at study, every year doing a bit better in class, working my way up from being bottom. Now, at the last hurdle, I was very much afraid my languages would let me down and ruin my chances of university.

Life at home went on much as before. Dad dropped me off at school then went onto his office. In his rooms at Tattersalls his clerk did the books and his other staff did the cash side. That meant that Dad was mostly being sociable or attending the various sports committees that he sat on. He would finish early and pick me up from school. It meant we got to chat as we went home which we both enjoyed. My parents were never worried how I would do. If anything they told me to ease off the study. They did not understand that, first, I had to study very hard to do well and, second, I wanted an education and an occupation I could rely on. I was not going to live on my wits.

Thank goodness, I got my matric. It was such a relief. My Latin must have brought my language marks up. That may sound surprising but I found Latin easier to learn than other languages because it has a very strict grammatic pattern. For example, one can work out the subject and object by the endings of the nouns and the verb always goes at the end.

When I got my matric I applied to read science at Pietermaritzburg where students read chemistry, physics and mathematics as major subjects. However, if a student did not get good enough marks in their language at matric then language had to be taken as a minor subject at university. As I feared, the English mark I got was too low. It meant that I would have to study language for three years and the very thought made me feel ill. It seemed a struggle too far to me at the time. I had had enough. The thought of studying English was keeping me awake at night and I could not stop worrying about it all day. I felt that if I did not get out of it, it would blight my time at university. I was obsessed. I put my every waking moment into coming up with a workable solution to avoid it. Eventually I decided that it all hinged on Mr Black, the headmaster. He was my only chance. Our marks were recorded on our subject papers and he had to sign them all. Only if my English mark was high enough would he sign the paper which gave me exemption from taking languages as an element of my degree. He taught me mathematics so he knew that was one of my best subjects but I reckoned that he may not have known about my language marks.

I settled on a strategy. I would have all my papers together, placing the science papers with the highest marks on the top and the paper with the low language mark last on the bottom of the pile. If I was lucky the headmaster would sign the first ones and – if the marks on the last one were not too apparent – he might automatically sign that too. If he did I would be home and dry. I would be able to concentrate on studying sciences as I wanted to.

Joining the other boys waiting outside the headmaster's study to go in and have their entry papers signed, I felt very apprehensive, extremely anxious. The boy before me came out. I felt sick to my stomach. I realised it was crazy to hope that he would not notice my low language mark. In I went. 'Well, Alexander,' said Mr Black in his loud voice, looking at me over his desk. 'Well done on your matriculation'. I stood in front of him. 'Thank you, Sir'. He had his pen poised. I put the papers down on the desk and held them in place while he signed the top one.

I picked them up, shuffled them, put them all down again and with the next one that needed signing on the top. And the same every time – he was doing them much faster now hardly looking at them - until the last language one which I kept half obscured by the better ones. My heart was making such a thumping noise that I was sure he could hear it. Everything went around in my head. If he did notice that my English mark was too low that was it. He would not sign it and I would have to study English for three more years and that could affect my whole degree. I held my breath.

To my horror he turned his pen up and looked at the nib. Had it run out of ink? This would give him time to check the papers and notice that the last one was not up to the mark. I felt sick. No, thank goodness, he righted the pen and signed. I kept my face very straight. I tried not to take the papers away too quickly. I held them in my hands behind my back. If they were not in his sight I was praying that they were out of his mind.

'And you have applied for Natal University College, is that correct?' 'Yes, Sir,' I answered looking straight ahead. 'To read for a Bachelor of Science degree?' 'Yes, Sir. That's right, Sir', I still did not dare look at him. 'Good, good, that's excellent', he said. He was already looking at his diary. 'Send the next boy in, will you Alexander?' 'Yes, Sir. Thank you, Sir', I said and turned towards the door. 'Oh, and Alexander?'

My chest constricted. My throat froze. I held my breath. Here we go, I thought. My shoulders slumped as I turned around to face him again. 'Yes, Sir?' I replied. I could barely hear my own voice. 'Good Luck'. 'Thank you, Sir', I said with such relief that I felt as if I would crumple to the ground. Instead, I turned, grasped the door handle and slipped out the door as smoothly and neatly as the most light-footed boxer could side-step a punch. Even Dad would have been proud of such a manoeuvre.

Once outside I slowed down, told the next boy to go in, walked down the passage with as measured step as I could manage and appearing calm to everyone around me went out the door. Then I ran and ran and ran waving my papers over my head until I got to the school gate, where I knew Dad would be waiting in the car for me. 'I've got it!' I shouted. 'I've got it! No more languages for me. Only science from now on – Yipee!'

And soon I was the proud owner of a matriculation certificate:
Durban High School
Joint Matriculation Certificate
Class II December 1934
English   Maths   Physics & Chemistry
Latin   Afrikaans   History
But I decided then and there that in future I would always aim and be in charge of my own study subjects because I never, ever, wanted to try such an anxiety inducing stunt again.

DHS 1932 : Eric, *standing 3rd row, centre*

13. How Asdic Works: Scotland, October 1941

Postcard of the Esplanade and Pier, Dunoon

U-boats are targeting our Atlantic convoys and are the biggest threat to our ships. They and their supply lines have to be kept open if we are to win this war. Max Horton, Admiral of the Western Approaches, insists that every escort of the Atlantic convoys should have at least two men trained to use Asdic. He is bent on destroying the U-boats. So, of course, the Admiralty has been as committed to improving the equipment. This is why we at Fairlie beaver away in a fight against the clock. But to do my bit to improve and modify the equipment I need to know how it is operated.

The naval ratings study the theoretical aspect of Asdic operation for two weeks at HMS *Osprey* in Dunoon, the anti-submarine detection shore base that was previously sited at Portland. After this they do a practical training course for submarine detection at HMS *Nimrod* based in Campbeltown. As well as listening for echoes, they practice listening to the sound of engines in the harbour to hone their ability to recognise different craft. Then they are put on the training ship, HMS *Nemesis*.

But intensive and rigorous though these courses are - using complicated convoy operation mock-ups called attack tables and every imaginable gadget to make the training realistic - these courses are really only introductory. Because, not until an operator is at sea, working with the equipment on the job, can he get the experience necessary. After some time at sea a number of operators attend the school again to do the advanced Asdic course.

Every cruiser and destroyer - and the corvettes, mine sweepers and frigates that escort the convoys - are fitted with Asdic. Each has a specific type fitted as do merchant ships. All craft are susceptible to U-boat attack or mine damage and the Asdic set is used to detect them.

The set uses an oscillator (for transmission and reception of underwater sound) which is mounted on the end of a vertical shaft that can be rotated and retracted. When it is lowered the set transmits and receives the echoes through a water filled stream-lined dome fitted to the hull of the ship. It is fitted below the water-line but avoiding the keel and is controlled from the Asdic hut. Originally these domes were made of canvas over a frame but now they are constructed of Staybright steel plates (which don't rust) with a small window through which the beam is directed. If such a dome is difficult to visualize imagine it is proportionately similar in size to that of a large pimple on somebody's nose.

The operating equipment is fitted in most vessels in an Asdic hut aft of the bridge, but in some newer vessels it is built in. How many operators man the Asdic equipment depends on the size of the vessel. In smaller vessels it could be manned by a lone operator. In larger vessels two or three operators, in which case it is the advanced Asdic operator who directs the search and does the calculations. A second operator reads out the bearing if an echo is heard. He is also the rating who controls the firing of the depth charges. If there is a third rating he will raise or lower the dome when there is insufficient depth.

An Asdic operator wears headphones to hear the incoming echoes. However, the operators tell me that they also have to hear what is going on around them and communicate with the Bridge. So they usually keep one headphone on and the other pulled aside. If the operator makes contact with a target, and Action Stations are then sounded, he can switch that headphone to transmit the echoes received through the loud speaker on the bridge so everyone keeps abreast of the status of alert.

Obviously, it would be impossible to search the sea at random for enemy submarines. Asdic cannot pick up U-boats at any range over 2000 yards. But, by using Asdic, ships hope to detect U-boats when they are nearby and likely to torpedo them. They can then target the U-boat before it attacks. The search procedure seems to be fairly standard. The operators are trained to set their range to so many yards (say 2000) and begin to search by sweeping sections listening intently for echoes. They say they usually start at Red (port) 30 degrees (most people know that port is the left side of a ship and I can always remember by repeating: Red port should be left) to perhaps 5 degrees past the bow. If no echo is heard on this bearing then the search would be from Green 30 degrees, and so on. By sweeping continuously in an arc the ship proceeds without worry of being torpedoed.

But if the operator thinks he has contact with a U-boat (hearing the ping which is the sound of the echo received back) he informs the Bridge. Generally, to avoid false alarms, he makes sure he has positive identification before he reports it, when he then gives the co-ordinates and assesses its type. If the target is large he may be able to keep contact easily and identify it. By speeding up his transmissions, and moving the oscillator only a degree at a time to get a better arc - a slow and regular ping, ping, ping - he can tell the length (he calls it the extent) of the target.

The operator informs the Captain of its echo bearing and estimates its range using a stop watch. He knows the speed of sound in water and calculates how long it takes from the time the sound wave was emitted to the time it gets back. From this he can tell how far away the U-boat is. Its range, in Naval speak. It's not a perfect system because obviously there is a small time lag whilst he does these calculations.

Diagram of Active Asdic Fan Shaped Beam Transmitted from Ship and Reflected Wave Received

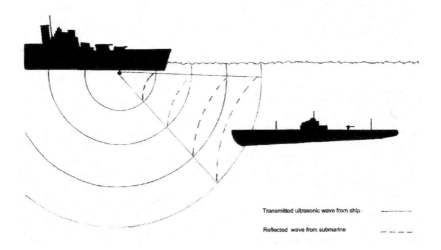

Transmitted ultrasonic wave from ship

Reflected wave from submarine

Doppler shift is the difference in frequency between an outgoing signal and the reflected echo. A change in pitch of the echo (apparently an experienced and highly trained operator can recognise this at once) means that the operator can tell if the target is moving towards the ship or away from it. If the emitted frequency of the transmission from the ship is returned higher from the target than it was sent, then the target is approaching the ship. If it is returned at a lower frequency, then the target is moving away from the ship. This is also known as the Doppler effect. A common physical demonstration might be to imagine a non-stopping passing train at a station. A train approaching the station makes a sound but as it passes the pitch of the sound changes. It sounds higher when it is coming towards the station and lower as it goes away from the station.

The Captain now knows the echo bearing of the target, its direction, range and, by its length, its estimated type. He makes the decision to attack - before the ship itself is torpedoed - and the ship changes its speed and possibly its course. The depth is estimated, the charges are armed and depth controls of the charges set. Alarm bells warn the crew to take up Action Stations. As the ship closes onto its target the operator hears constant fast pinging. But, as it gets within range of firing, the equipment can no longer pick up an echo. It is too close.

The Asdic cannot detect the U-boat when it is close because the cone-shaped oscillator beam is fixed on the ship at 10 degrees below the horizontal. When the ship is, say, 1000 yards from the target, and the target is at a depth of 400 feet, the U-boat would be detected by the beam. However, when a ship is very close to the target, say 200 yards, and the target is 400 feet deep, it is below the beam and cannot be tracked.

Asdic contact is still lost as the ship passes quickly over the target, or the U-boat passes behind the Asdic beam. The firing signal is given and depth charges are dropped from the platform over the stern. Blind time - the time between losing contact and the depth charge reaching its target - can be anything from 45 to 90 seconds. From the controls the operator can turn the oscillator round 180 degrees to transmit dead astern and, if he is sensible, he removes his headphone to save his eardrums from a battering. The ship will still be close enough to feel the blast but not be damaged. If the surface of the sea rises signalling that the charges have hit their target - and providing there are no survivors to pick up - the ship sails on and the operator begins his sweep ahead once more.

This is the text-book *modus operandi*. However, it does not happen like this often enough. Surfaced U-boats in increasing numbers are hunting our convoys using their Radar and it is usual that they detect our ships before we find them as the range of our Asdic is limited. But it can happen that a U-boat is taken unawares when hunting submerged close to a convoy and, caught in the Asdic sweep, it tries to avoid detection. However, sooner or later it knows that it has been detected and inevitably, as soon as the U-boat knows it is possibly about to be attacked, it reacts. It is at the stage when the hunter ship loses Asdic contact (blind time) that a U-boat can take evasive action. It is aware that within a hundred yards of the sub the equipment on the ship will not be able to pinpoint it. It either quickly changes course and escapes out of range or dives deep enough to avoid a hit. The smartest U-boat commanders have a whole raft of tricks they use to dodge detection.

To state the obvious, a lone ship fitted with Asdic is small and the ocean is large. A lone ship detecting an enemy submarine is like looking for a grain of sand in a bath full of water. Although it does happen that a solitary ship detects a U-boat and goes in pursuit, more often than not the German submarine is spotted by an RAF plane (and here their Radar is improving enormously) which alerts the ship that can then go in for the kill.

It is far less likely that a U-boat will avoid detection if our ships are in convoy as the vessels in convoy are positioned so that their Asdic beams produce an overlapping coverage. But, the fact remains that however many ships are involved, depth charges that can only be dropped close to a target are not the most effective weapon. Most enemy losses are due to multiple depth charges being dropped rather than accurate positioning.

So, even after detection, there are inherent shortcomings with our anti-submarine devices. First, because Asdic cannot get an echo from a submerged U-boat at very close range and loss of contact occurs there is a chance for the target to escape (or possibly release a torpedo). Second, Asdic sets have no depth finding capability so operators can only guess at what depth the depth charge should explode. Thirdly, because calculations to pinpoint the target are not done automatically, valuable seconds are lost. And, finally, Asdic operators need to be better trained and officers need to learn how to counter the tricks used by U-boats to avoid detection.

Before the war there was a naval agreement between Germany and

Britain so we were aware in which direction their submarine research was going. When the war started we therefore knew that German scientists had concentrated on developing passive listening detection devices such as hydrophones whilst we tended to concentrate on active ultrasonic echo-ranging research and equipment.

A U-boat captured earlier this year was examined here at Fairlie and the sophistication of their detection devices was apparently clear to see. It was agreed that the German success in hunting our convoys is at least partly due to the fact that their submarine listening range using a multi-hydrophone system of detection is performing in a superior manner and at a much greater range than our ships' standard Asdic set can achieve. They are detecting us before we are detecting them and, even if we do detect them, our Asdic sets have shortcomings that could result in terrible losses.

There is no doubt, then, that our Asdic sets must be improved and I can now see that there are several areas where it could be done. All of us scientists, engineers and technicians working on submarine echo-detection at Fairlie are trying to achieve this. Achieve it we must, in record time, if we are to help stem the loss of our fleet and save lives.

14. Hedgehogs: Scotland, November – December 1941

Postcard of Largs from the South East

I really feel one of the team now that I'm thoroughly getting to grips with oscillator research and modification of Asdic equipment. Vig, who's a metrologist (that's the study of exact time) and physicist, is head of Anti-Submarine Research (that's us) which deals with oscillator development, sound measurements and so on. Although we have several teams here all with different areas of expertise on Asdic our paths cross constantly. Little of our research is in total isolation and I thoroughly enjoy the feeling that we are all working together in one common cause.

Every research scientist here deals with the Experiment and Development department, Tony Law's large section, which produces and develops the equipment and Asdic sets. It's where Bob Gamble and Morgan are busy developing the latest modifications to recorder equipment whilst Rick Dawson and Law work on the latest mortars and depth charges. Law co-ordinates all the development (it's all sent down to Bath to be made) but it's down to Dering to make sure that everything is compatible with ship fitting.

It was when Anti-Submarine Detection section was at HMS *Osprey* at Portland that all these chaps first started to work on Smith's idea of an ahead-thrown anti-submarine weapon. It was a projectile light enough in weight to be fitted on to almost any vessel. Big advantage. Dawson did the operational research and it was fully developed up here and became known as the 'Fairlie Mortar'. Made up of two sets of ten mortar barrels it threw 20lb depth charges in a circular pattern ahead of the ship.

However, as alternative depth charge throwers are being developed at other Establishments, Smith's has been rejected as too ineffectual. This happened soon after I arrived here. It seems that Smith felt it was discontinued for the wrong reasons (he means not scientific ones) so he is making a real stink. Fortunately, I was warned early on otherwise I might have made one of my puns to Smith about the mortar being dropped. A joke that would have gone down like a lead balloon.

At the same time, Law was doing the experimental work on speeding up sinking times of depth charges to try and ameliorate the blind time during an attack when Asdic contact is lost. The faster the depth charge sinks the less time the sub has to escape. The trials for his early versions came to nothing and now his latest idea of a single, very large depth charge designed to be dropped off the stern rails is also likely to come to nothing. Like Smith's mortar, it has been overtaken this year by the development of a much more effective anti-submarine ahead-thrown weapon known as the Hedgehog.

The Hedgehog is a multi-spigot mortar that will be fitted onto the deck of destroyers and corvettes. The destroyers are in hand for fitting but it seems that the corvettes will need further modification so they will take longer. The weapon has twenty-four projectiles, fitted with fuses that can be fired two at a time at fraction of a second intervals.

They are thrown a-head of the ship (which is why the weapon has been called the Head-gehog) in a ring pattern. All in all, it does seem to be quite an improvement on the depth charge. Not that I would risk saying so in front of anyone from Experiment and Development.

The Hedgehog will mean that blind time is greatly reduced; 15-20 seconds instead of 45-90 seconds − a big difference. Morgan is busy adapting the range recorder to use with it and Gamble is working on a bearing recorder. As the ship approaches an enemy submarine ahead, the range recorder will show when the correct range is reached (about 250 yards ahead of the ship) as well as the time to fire. Meanwhile - if it works as planned - the bearing recorder will record the movement of the submarine and, with the help of a gyro, indicate the course on paper for the ship's Captain to steer. Presently (with only the range recorder) the operator has to judge by eye. It will be so much more reliable and precise with both recorders.

There are other advantages. Less time lag, for a start. More chance of a kill with multiple charges fired in a pattern than with a single very large charge. Also projectiles with contact fuses will get over the problem that our Asdic cannot yet determine the depth of the target. Now, this is where I come in. A new Asdic set for destroyers, Type 144, was conceived at Fairlie this summer. It is being developed to use with the recorders and Hedgehog.

The oscillators used in it can create a search beam (shaped like a submarine funnily enough) capable of long-range detection. It uses the standard 15inch diameter oscillator operating at 19Kc/s. I have started to do some experimental research on the oscillators used in it to determine the depth of the target and it's a case of modification, refinement and improvement after every trial. It has fallen to me to write up the reports of the results of our trials and this is sent every week to the Admiralty to be typed up and circulated to the fleet so they can make use of it. I feel honoured to be entrusted with all this and to be so thoroughly involved.

The work is so intense that everyone is glad to switch off now and then. There may not be many public places of entertainment but everyone is very welcoming and tries to lay on what they can. Newton William-Powlett and his wife, 'Call me Barbara', have invited me to dinner for a second time. They are very civilized and Barbara, who is only about ten years older than me, is a really good sport. Likes my jokes and doesn't groan too much at my puns. Says they need all the levity they can get up here in the north. The Scots don't get annoyed when she says that because she's honest enough to admit that it's as isolated where she lives down in the Devon sticks. But we quietly agree that the weather up here can get you down.

One of the W-P's children, Sarah - who I suppose is about six - is very taken with me. I made an origami bird for her when I went there the first time and now I get no peace until I produce one for her and another for her sister. If only I could find and impress a nice girlfriend as easily. This time I am asked by Barbara and the other women if I can make anything else, which stretches my memory a bit. I say birds are actually my speciality, which has them all laughing.

At a social supper the way the war is going is touched on as little as possible. Of course, everyone here is primarily concerned with the Battle of the Atlantic. But they like to forget the horror stories for a while so they also keep up with what's going on elsewhere. The campaign in Africa is one. When they hear my accent, which I think is slight, the only non-war story they can think of that's associated with Africa is the sensational death of Lord Errol.

He has been shot through the back of the head in Kenya. 'Is that what life was like for you', they ask. 'All drinking, gambling and adultery?' I think of my parents and their life in Africa. Drinking and gambling went on a lot. And probably adultery for all I know. But no-one I knew shot anyone as a result of it. Nor was it as giddy or glamorous as they make it sound. But everyone around the table wants to be safely shocked so I don't commit myself, merely raise my eyebrows and give a big grin and everyone laughs, believing what they want.

My father thought it incumbent on one to be as entertaining as possible at a dinner party particularly in mixed company and so I keep up the thrilling history of Africa by mentioning that my grandfather was killed at the Battle of Isandhlwana in 1879. Everyone wants to hear the details. From Ireland apparently, he joined the British Army. He fought in the Crimean War and in India, was discharged from the army and retired to the Cape with his family. As he could ride and shoot straight he joined the Natal Mounted Police because he was still young and had a large family to keep.

When the British Army needed more troops to cross into Zululand he volunteered to go upcountry with them. Lord Chelmsford left 1,500 of these troops camped on the hill at Isandhlwana. But they failed to laager their wagons and were taken by surprise when they were attacked by 20,000 Zulus. Nearly every soldier was killed at the Battle of Isandlwana and my grandfather was amongst the last to die fighting. Their ammunition boxes were screwed shut and the men could not open them in the heat of the battle and were all shot, or speared, or both.

This story has always drawn surprise from anyone I have told it to and this occasion was no exception. However, because this was a mixed dinner party I thought it insensitive to add the family story that my grandfather's eldest son found his father's body with his heart cut out and put in his mouth. Which is what the Zulus do to release the spirit of the dead man.

In the labs we now discuss something quite new. Depth determination. An alternative completely new design of oscillator is required for attachments to the Type 144 that we hope will finally be able to determine depth. We are keeping it very hush, hush. George and Alex are in my team again. Everything is stations go. We are all very aware what a race it is to beat those damn U-boats before they beat us.

Suddenly something surprising happens that sends alarm bells ringing in the Admiralty and the Navy. Human torpedoes, undetected by the Harbour Defence Asdic (HDA), have attacked and damaged some of our ships in a Mediterranean port. HDA are Asdic that can be placed on the sea bed - or to the breakwater at the entrance to the harbour - to detect vessels entering. Two of our research scientists, Dr. Hector Willis and his wife, Marie, (both physicists from ARL) concentrate here on HDA.

Fortunately, the Establishment had been forewarned that the Italians had a miniature craft able to breach this type of defence. The Willis' had therefore already started improving the HDA (Type 135) to better detect smaller craft like human torpedoes or midget submarines entering ports.

As they share an office with Vig in R&D I see quite a bit of them. Willis has already enlisted my help with his project and we get on very well. Marie, who is very motherly towards me, invited me to their house for a meal as soon as I arrived. Marie loves her flower garden and Hector his vegetables. On Sundays I help them dig their vegetable patch to give me some exercise and they reward me with a slap-up meal. A large roast and home-grown veggies are not in Mrs. Hutton's remit.

Marie Willis in her garden

Then, at the start of December, more startling news still. Japan attacks the U.S. base in Pearl Harbour! We are all a bit shocked. Japan's allies are Italy and Germany. They will be in it together. A few days later Hitler declares war on the U.S. This means that the Americans are in the war now. Terrible news for them, wonderful news for us. At the Establishment we all feel that this country has a chance at last and our mood really lifts. America's bad luck is our good luck. After all our losses and worries surely - we tell each other - with their military support we can indeed win this war. Christmas may not be so bad after all.

The Hedgehog has been a success for us this year and whenever the mortar is mentioned I involuntarily think of the little animal that I often unearth in the Willis' garden. It is always a pleasure to find one as I am immediately reminded of all the pets I had throughout my childhood and how I had enjoyed collecting everything zoological. And the great fun I had creating and adapting all manner of items and potions in order to keep or preserve them. It was, perhaps, the start of my interest in chemistry.

15. My Museum: South Africa, 1932

Postcard of Ocean Beach, Marine Parade, Durban

My mother hated the flat. We had been living on Marine Parade for about a year after Mom and I returned from our long holiday in Australia. I loved it because I could wander along the promenade, fish off the pier, go into town whenever I wanted or surf in the ocean with other boys who lived nearby. We would go far - outside the safety of the shark free enclosure – wait for a very large slide and ride right into the water's edge. It was thrilling. But Mom, on the other hand, said that she felt hemmed in and so spent her time out playing cards. Inevitably she lost money and that resulted in my parents quarrelling more than usual. One morning at breakfast Mom said, 'This really won't do, Phillip, I'm bored. I need something to do. Something to keep me occupied.'

It was well known that my mother was an excellent cook and the family said that she had run the hospitality side of Cape Town theatres very efficiently. A short while later, perhaps with this in mind, Dad told

Mom that he had bought her an hotel and said to me, 'It will keep your mother out of mischief'. So we moved out of the flat and into The Lowther Hotel, just off West Street, opposite the Majestic. On the ground floor there was a palm court – an inner courtyard open to the sky – above which were bedrooms with verandas that looked down on it. Most of the guests liked to sit and have their meals in the courtyard rather than in the dining room. The wicker tables and chairs there were moved under the verandas when it rained.

Mom no longer had time to play cards as both she and Dad were too busy with the hotel. He rose early and opened the public bar at six o'clock. It was at the side of the hotel and opened on to the street. The workmen called in there on their way to work for a quick tot - brandy and milk usually – and he served them because they could be a bit rough. They knew Dad had won prizes for boxing so they behaved themselves when he was there.

When the barmaid came in at eight o'clock Dad went to the office. He usually took a rickshaw as he said it was quicker and more convenient than the car. Mom was in sole charge then. She supervised the Indian cooks we had but if she fancied something they did not make, or would not make, she cooked it herself and she ran the guest bar on the upper floor. Wine for the bar was bought in barrels and we bottled it. Sometimes I helped which involved going down into the cellar and pouring the wine through a funnel into the bottles. My particular job was to pull the handle on the contraption that corked them.

The extra space available in the hotel did mean that I could have a room especially for my collections, where my Alsatian dog, Rex, kept me company. I started collecting when I was six or so. Mom and Dad's friends called me *Inkosaan* or the Little Professor then because I was always collecting, finding out about my specimen or working out how to preserve them. It was always referred to as 'my museum', something that many boys had then.

To preserve insects I used a special screw topped jar to knock them out. In the bottom was an inch of sawdust, then a paste with plaster of

Paris and water was poured on top to a depth of about one inch. Before the plaster set I made several holes in it. Finally, ethyl acetate was poured into the jar which trickled through the holes and was absorbed by the sawdust. When the insect was put into the jar and the lid done up, it died very quickly from the fumes. I remember Mom making me a net to catch butterflies and these I displayed. This required mounting them with pins on setting boards approximately one foot long with a groove down the middle. Whilst squeezing the thorax between my thumb and first finger, I pushed a darning needle stuck into a wine bottle cork through it. A difficult process to carry out without damaging the delicate wings. Then the mounting pin was put through the hole and stuck in the board.

Of course I had the usual vegetation and geological stuff in my collection. Pods, seeds and leaves were dried or pressed. Fossils, ammonites, arrowheads, special stones and pebbles were amassed. And I loved my piece of amethyst, which is the crystalline quartz found in granite. I also had a live collection of silkworms, stick insects, spiders and slow worms. And a wet collection - these were specimen preserved in ethyl alcohol or, if I had none, in my parent's vodka.

When I was about fourteen I preserved a python skin, an easy enough thing to do if one had enough strength. The python was slit top to tail and the skin peeled off. This was then scraped clean of flesh, stretched out, pinned to a board and dried. It was then necessary to treat it to preserve it. Mixing alum powder (the stuff my Dad used on his mouth ulcers and Mom used making her pickles) with coarse salt and a little oil it was spread on the skin. More of the mixture had to be applied over the next few days until the skin was quite dry. Ten days usually did it. Some boys at school sold their python skins to the Snake Park (to be made into handbags and so on) but I hung onto mine to build up a comprehensive selection in my collection.

The men who lived in the hotel – Mom called them The Old Soaks because they drank all day long whilst they played cards - were always very interested in what I did. They would ask me about my projects but they would also teach me all sorts of things. At one point one of them gave me a chess lesson every day after school and another taught me how to make various origami animals. They also told me wonderful stories and the one I liked best at the time was the one about the drunk. One of their fellow residents played for the Durban orchestra as a trombonist. He was a nice chap but got drunk every night after the performance. When he returned to the hotel he always asked for two bottles of stout to be opened which he took to bed with him. He drank one and put the other on the floor next to his bed so he could drink it in the morning before he got up.

Apparently, one night, he returned more than usually the worse for wear, ordered his stout as normal and put it down beside his bed next to his boots. He was so drunk that he was still tipsy the next morning and poured his stout into his boot by mistake. But, not to be put off, he picked up the boot up and drank the stout anyway!

The zoo snake keeper

My collection had taken years to amass and perfect but my favourite item remained something I had from the age of about nine, a monkey skull. After a while I decided that I would like the skull to be animated. If the jaw of the monkey moved it would look 'alive' and after experimenting I worked out how to achieve it. The skull was mounted on a stick. Then I wired the two parts of the jaw so they hinged on each side. An elastic band was attached to the jaw and by moving the stick the jaw lifted up and down.

When I also wiggled the stick it really looked like the monkey skull was biting or chattering. If anyone came into my museum uninvited I moved the stick without them noticing and the monkey's jaw opened and closed. It gave people – girls especially - a terrible surprise which, as any boy knows, is a very amusing thing to do. The playing of practical jokes was something I never grew out of and, during my working life, I met many Naval officers who enjoyed them as much as myself.

16. Sitting Ducks:
Scotland, December 1941 – March 1942

Postcard of Loch Striven and Bute

I go down to London for Christmas and my mother is very pleased to see me. Nevertheless, within minutes she takes me to task over the state of my tweed jacket. She is so fussy about appearances that she even goes so far as to offer me some of her coupons to put towards a new one. I say I have no intention of ditching this jacket as it saw me through the coldest winter in Oxford and will be well and truly needed in this coming Scottish winter. I could tell she was relieved.

From somewhere she has managed to acquire some leather elbow patches and when I am in bed she sows them on. I am quizzed about everything in Scotland but as I can't talk about work I have to keep changing the subject and ask what she is up to. Hearing about all her trials and tribulations I nevertheless notice the pile of theatre programmes has grown considerably and that her little diary, when she gets it out of her handbag to write down the cost of the elbow patches with the tiny pencil, is very full. The only thing I have found to spend money on since I started work has been to buy a new camera that I can use to take transparencies so – having treated myself – I tell her that I will be able to start repaying her some of what I owe her for my years at Oxford out of my salary each month.

If I was for even one moment thinking she might suggest it could come out of Dad's estate, I would have been greatly mistaken. Very matter of factly, she says a cheque in January would be very useful and that the next time I come she will sow on some leather binding to cover up the fraying showing on the cuffs. I imagine that this too will go into the little account page of her diary.

Recalling all those years when my mother spent money like water – distributing largess to her friends and putting up champagne for everyone - I find the change in her attitude very marked. Being careful with money and anxious about finances has come on her with widowhood and middle age. Perhaps it is fear of a return to the hard years of her childhood or the insecurity of owning no property. Here's hoping that my education will give me security. I want no fortune to make or to lose, only a well-paid job and a good pension.

Having planned a quick trip to Oxford I leave her on the day after Boxing Day getting dolled up to go out for a game of Bridge. Making my way off to the railway station I am aware that my shiny new elbow patches might be drawing attention to the faded, lumpy old age of the jacket to which they are attached. And as I hurry along I am sad to see the iron railings and gates – scrap needed for armaments - coming down around the streets and squares. I remember as a boy the pleasure of walking, stick in hand, clattering along the railings until an adult caught me at it and told me off.

Margot was also pleased to see me – and I her – and we have a day of fun trying out my new camera in all our old haunts. I cannot wait to see the transparencies. Our sex life back on track, I leave her in Oxford and return to London to go back up north. It seems that every service man on leave also wants to travel up there and the throng on the station platform is huge. The train will be over crowded as usual and I shall be extremely lucky to get a seat. In war time train journeys are terrible at the best of times so I hate to think what it will be like when there are American service men travelling too. Every passenger is hampered by not only their luggage but also a gas mask hung over their shoulder. Every soldier, sailor and airman has, added to that, a tin hat and often a water bottle plus all their kit. I have decided I must get a haversack which I can put on my back because even my small leather case is impossible to manoeuvre through these crowds. In the meantime I have taken to carrying my case African style, holding it with two hands on my head. I am taller than most people so manage to get through the crowded platform a bit easier.

Once on the train I am very quick, nab a seat and wedge my case out of the way in the overhead luggage rack. The service men pack the carriages and sit on the floor of the passages, their kitbags lying in wait for anyone rash enough to try and stretch their legs. Fortunately I have managed to rig myself up with some sausage rolls, a couple of sandwiches and a slice of cake. I will only take essential sips from my thermos flask of tea because I'm not leaving my seat for anything. The only good thing about the crowded and tedious journey are the jokes I hear from the men. I have a good chuckle and it gives me an excellent supply for the chaps when I get back. Although I will have to clean some of them up.

If it wasn't for the weather I would say that I was thoroughly glad to get back to Scotland and work. Not only are the skies wide and views of the heather covered hills so much more liberating than any city landscape but since I have been asked to focus on oscillator research I have found the work more interesting as every day goes by. The experimental high frequency oscillator set (Type 144) for depth determination has done well in the trials up here on Loch Striven. But trials in the choppier waters of the open sea have not done as well so stabilizing gear is being fitted. Once that is done I shall be able to see how it performs aboard HMS *Kingfisher*, the corvette that we use for deep sea trialing.

When we hear that a U-boat has been sunk by Hedgehog there are cheers and a real feeling of achievement. Generally, however, this winter and spring have been a frustrating time for the Royal Navy and especially for the RAF. First, in early February, the RAF has to withdraw from our major military base in Singapore leaving Allied troops with no air cover. This is followed by the disastrous news that Japan has captured Singapore taking thousands of prisoners. What a blow. Then there is yet more bad news. The RAF suffers severe losses nearer home.

In 1940 the giant German battlecruiser, KMS *Scharnhorst,* sank our cruiser, HMS *Rawalpindi,* and then, together with her sister ship KMS *Gneisenau,* sank our aircraft carrier, HMS *Glorious,* off Norway. Since then she has regularly raided our merchant ships. Understandably we want her sunk. Sitting ducks in the French port of Brest, *Scharnhorst, Gneisenau* and the heavy cruiser, KMS *Prinz Eugen,* have been subject to repeated bombing raids by the RAF but, unfortunately, none of them successful. In an attempt to escape back to Germany they have made a daring dash up the English Channel and back to their ports without being sunk by either our coastal forces, ships or bombers.

The German ships suffered surprisingly little damage but our forces were not so lucky. There were substantial RAF and Fleet Air Arm losses and a humiliating defeat for the Royal Navy. To allow enemy ships to pass through the English Channel and so close to land is unimaginable and terrifying. It has cast a pall over everything and everyone. The only thing we can console ourselves with is that the German ships will no longer threaten our Atlantic convoys from Brest. But time will tell what they get up to next.

When I turn 26 it is my only evening off for weeks. Somehow a birthday is not what it was and a couple of beers are the only celebration I have. That and a jumper knitted by my mother. How times have changed. To try and prize me away from the lab George has browbeaten me into joining the amateur dramatic troupe here at the Establishment.

Apparently, it is a good antidote to war, worry and work. The players call themselves *The Supersonics*. I've agreed because there are one or two pretty girls in the cast and there are few other chances to socialize in Fairlie. It's home grown entertainment or nothing at all. There will be two performances of the play - in Largs then West Kilbride - which sounds quite ambitious.

We meet a couple of times a week and I have to admit it is quite a lark. I have a walk-on part as a policeman in a bowler hat and don't have to say a word. Perhaps the producer is afraid a South African accent will slip out. But, as it happens, not having to learn lines suits me down to the ground. My brain is still reeling from all that's going on here. Everything we do regarding research has a high degree of security attached to it. Classified, Confidential, Secret or Top Secret stamped on one or other. I don't get to see the Most Secret. I am now working on a new miniature Asdic set that I am fully aware the Germans must never get wind of. This one will be for a very specific craft, due to carry out a top secret mission, of which only a few of us here have only been allowed to hear the most basic details in order to develop our design. At other Establishments different parts of the puzzle are no doubt being developed.

At nearby bases training is always evolving; there are several of them here in Scotland. Across the Firth of Clyde, at the Royal Navy submarine base at Holy Loch, north of Dunoon, the subs come up to be fitted with torpedoes. The loch is used extensively for exercises and we use it for further trials as it is considered very safe due to the boom built across the estuary between Dunoon and Cloch Point to defend the water from German U-boats. At Helensburgh on Gareloch destroyers come up to be fitted with anti-submarine equipment. And it is at here that the RN shore establishment known as HMS *Vernon,* discreetly sited in lovely old houses, has its mining school.

Also at Port Bannantyne is a small de-gaussing range and a floating dock for ship repairs. Degaussing is something one tends to only know about if in the Navy. All vessels have a magnetic pull that can be detected by enemy craft. In the case of ships, 'degaussing' coils can be fitted aboard which supply a direct current to generate their own magnetic fields designed to oppose the ship's magnetization. But de-gaussing is a real problem for submarines because coils cannot be permanently fitted to the outside of them to reduce or camouflage magnetization. It's something we're working on.

Sonobuoys are another anti-submarine device I am working on. A sonar buoy is basically a listening device – powered by a battery and fitted with an oscillator and radio transmitter - that floats on the surface of the water and detects by means of sound waves when a submarine (or a ship) comes into range. It then transmits this acoustic information to the receiving ship (possibly one of those in a convoy) or aircraft. This sausage shaped piece of kit – approximately six foot in length - is either dropped overboard into the ocean from a ship or dropped from an aircraft. It submerges so that only its radio transmitter floats on the surface of the water.

The buoys at present dropped and towed behind convoy ships to detect whether a U-boat is in range can also be used to confuse the U-boat that the sound it emits is that of the ship. Tests are showing that these buoys do detect submarines and can confuse the U-boat that the ship is elsewhere but there are limitations: their battery life is limited, so too is their lifetime use and the hydrophones fitted in them are only one directional, whilst the sound of a submarine can be difficult to hear over the noise of the ocean. These are the factors that I and others – in tandem with the Americans – will be trying to improve on.

Quite a few Norwegians work on all these bases now. They escaped after the Germans occupied Norway in April 1940 and found their way to Britain. This year many have made the dangerous journey across the North Sea to Shetland in the smallest of Norwegian fishing boats. Not all of them made it. Some of the well qualified Norwegian captains now pilot our merchant ships on coastal duties to free up the British captains. Also, at HMS *Osprey*, a few of the Norwegian naval officers teach our ratings how to use the Asdic equipment. Because they have been trained how to use oscillators on ships and are very good at it. But three officers, Nordtvedt, Engelsen and their Lieutenant Commander, work here at the Establishment. Not on the experimental side but on tactical issues. They are billeted at Fairlie Burn along with our single RN officers and some of the Establishment bachelor scientists like Vig.

KMS *Tirpitz*, one of the largest if not the largest German battleship, is another sitting duck in the Norwegian fjords posing a threat to our convoys. The RAF has attempted another attack on it. Unfortunately, this time it was not only unsuccessful but pilots' lives were lost. Things are not looking good. Even the large, four-engine bomber — the Lancaster — that has lately come into service did not perform as well as the RAF hoped. Nevertheless, we are still hopeful the Lancaster will come up to standard and so make a difference. We all badly need some successes.

17. On Board: Scotland, April - June 1942

Postcard of HMS *Penzance*, lost September 1940.

The Americans have at last realised the threat that U-boats pose. Our merchant ships and cargo vessels coming across the Atlantic, as well as those on their way to the Northern ports, have to be escorted to protect them from U-boat attack. Otherwise food supplies would never get through to us from America and weapons and other supplies from Britain would never reach our Allies. But the U.S. has rejected our system of convoys to minimise losses and has not applied it to their own merchant fleet. As a result they have suffered high shipping losses on their Eastern seaboard.

Naval officers of theirs who have been attached to the R.N. over here for some time appreciated it long ago but the powers in the U.S. were deaf, dumb and blind to the threat. However, it seems that their top brass have swallowed their pride and the U.S. Navy is now interested in escorts and convoys and in particular the anti-submarine detection devices we use on them. In fact, they want one of the principal scientists here to visit the U.S. to explain how we carry out our anti-submarine research. It's not been decided yet who can be spared to go. They are also asking if the Commander from HMS *Osprey* can go too, to advise on training. They have finally accepted that we know what we're doing. But we cannot afford to be smug because this year we ourselves have been having a hard time with U-boats sinking far too many of our ships.

The old guard here at the Establishment tell me that the Americans copy our stuff then make the mistake of trying to improve on it. Obviously, there is nothing wrong with trying to improve on a design or a system. It is what we scientists do. Scientific research is often not about discovering something new as most people think but more usually about discovering what we do not know about a product or process. A negative result can prove to be a positive benefit. By looking critically at how something functions – or learning from its possible failure – one may be able to work out how to overcome that malfunction and hopefully improve on the original. It is very often by small steps and not by big leaps that scientific progress is made.

The Americans have tried to improve on our attack table and the chemical range recorder and even the streamlined dome. But all of these were functioning well. Had they known the painstaking trial and error that went into the original - and everything we do here - they might have realised that we had already gone through the process. So it often happens that after their adaptions, they find that the gear does not work so well.

Whenever this occurs it seems that we have to send someone over to Canada or the States to explain it or supervise manufacture. On the other hand, no-one over here can deny that production is something at which the Americans are excellent. That and supplies. In the event Eric Pratt is 'spared' to explain our anti-submarine research. He is certainly a senior research scientist (not simply because he's getting on a bit) because over ten years ago he was working on new designs for quartz oscillators with Pew at Portland, now in Ottawa himself supervising the manufacture of Asdic equipment. The Canadians make it for us there and also supply it to the U.S. Navy.

The Admiralty has decided it needs some way to exchange information regarding anti-submarine warfare with the U.S. Navy and has set up an Anti-Submarine Division of the British Admiralty Delegation (BAD) in Washington, as the technical arm of the Naval Attache's job. Whoever is in charge there is the link between the U.S. Navy and the Royal Navy and has to not only represent every technical department of the Royal Navy but understand Asdic sets and other anti-submarine gear being fitted in British ships in the U.S. Accordingly it is through BAD that we exchange information about our latest gear.

Fortunately, the trials on HMS *Kingfisher* for the depth determining Asdic (Type 144) have been successful and it is now about to go into service. It will be a great help with submarine detection. Presently, whilst we are fully occupied designing attachments to enhance the new set, we are briefed on something else.

The very specific single unit oscillators we are developing especially for the highly classified top secret application are coming along. Everything is test and trial, test and trial. But as the trials for the prototype craft are completed we have got to keep abreast. It is a great responsibility but the excitement here amongst us on the research side is positively electric. It may be because we are all young and enthusiastic or because we have simply so many ideas buzzing around in our heads. Someone suggests one thing, that sparks off an alternative from another scientist, an engineer refines the design and we all scurry off to see if it stands up. Our every waking hour is spent on either this or some other high priority gear.

The Germans are now building U-boats at a faster rate that we are building destroyers and it is less and less likely that more than one escort vessel or destroyer can track each U-boat. So it is essential that our submarine detection devices are in good working order and do their job. I get several panic calls now to sort out Asdics on ships at sea that are not functioning properly. It usually follows a pattern.

First the call, 'Dr Alexander, do you think you could sort out an Asdic set that's not functioning?' I'm used to this. 'Have the electrical chappies on board had a look at it?' I ask. I've been out too often only to find that something simple was the reason, like the outer casing was not earthed. 'Yes, but they can't fathom it out. Off the Irish coast, operator takes a sweep and nothing.' I probe a bit more, 'What about the maintenance base staff, what do they say?' It's a long way to go if it's not strictly necessary and wastes valuable time. 'The A/S MO (I know most of these abbreviations by now; that's the Anti-Submarine Maintenance Officer) reports that the apparatus left port fully functioning. There's no-one there able to come out and she can't get underway till it's working properly. Has a convoy to join.'

'Alright,' I say, after all this is an emergency, can't hold a convoy up, 'I'll leave right away.' 'Good, my officers will get your transport sorted.' For trials and eventualities like this I've taken to keeping my small leather suitcase in the lab. So I don't waste time going home for my kit. Only a toothbrush and razor, an old pair of pyjamas, change of pants and socks. In case I'm stuck there overnight. Also a heavy woollen jumper. I take my college scarf and my mackintosh with me of course. It's pretty damn cold here in the winter but it can be blowing a gale out there in the Atlantic at any time. I don't take any equipment or tools. Apart from the tiny screwdriver and a pencil I keep in my top pocket. It's usually only my brain I'm using.

The launch collects me from Fairlie Pier and takes me out to the ship. It's a patrol craft, I prefer something a bit larger for longer distances but it's not so far this time and there is only me. As soon as I board the destroyer the Captain greets me and I go straight to the Asdic hut. The senior operator explains. Two ratings and myself go to the compartment that has the hatch to the dome, enter and lock ourselves in. One of them unbolts the hatch and it takes both of them (the equipment weighs about 400 pounds) to hoist up the directing shaft —

which is about 6 foot long - to which the oscillator is attached. The 20 Kc/s oscillator- twelve inches across - is encased in a rubber skin and fitted into a metal case with a Staybright window. Before I do anything I examine the rubber casings on the oscillator. There is looseness. On closer inspection I realise that the connectors to the oscillators are not fitted correctly causing feedback. The tightening rings at the back have not been tightened sufficiently and there was leakage from transmissions.

It is forbidden for any rating or officer to take a set apart. Security is tight because the design of the oscillators must never leak to the Germans. Which is the reason why I'm here. This time I manage to put things right and tighten the rings. But before now I've found that it is simply something that has worked loose. Perhaps it has taken a knock. I explain to the operators that the set is equipment that must be treated with utmost care. They must handle it as if they were carrying a very full pint of beer from the bar. They lower the hoist as if their lives depend on it. Which, of course, might be true.

I go up to report to the Captain. The operators look resigned, the Captain relieved. But I don't even have time for a good steaming mug of tea as they want to be underway immediately. Within minutes I have shaken hands with him and boarded the patrol craft again. Making for home. It's a long way to come to find that it was something simple that Maintenance should have done. I think about it and decide that, in all fairness, these sets are new, the operators inexperienced and the maintenance chaps so overworked that it is not surprising.

But even a small failure in the equipment can be significant so must be investigated. It is an opportunity to fine tune or correct gear that may make all the difference. I decide that the design could do with a tweak. This is the benefit of seeing the equipment in action. Just a simple remedy to stop cables working loose, for example. So, on my way home, I get my ideas down before I forget. The solution must be something that can be used on every set that has been fitted. It must also be installed in those being assembled. It cannot be anything that will change the production line or the arrangement of components. Nothing that will take any time. In these cases, as soon as I'm back, I take my sketch along to Jo Davis, the engineer in charge of Design, and we talk through the problem. Since I have been so closely involved in oscillator research I have to attend the official monthly progress meetings with the other research scientists. For ease of reporting and security we are all referred to as our code name on paper: Paul Vigoureux is R, Research; Willis, Research 1; Ben Browne, R2; Jackson, R3; Emerson, R4; Handley, R5 and I am RO, Research Oscillators. I now get a much broader picture and hear all sorts of interesting facts and ideas.

The Admiralty reckon that a scientist has his most creative years before he is thirty-eight years old and a mathematician is at his most productive when he's twenty-eight. I don't know how they arrived at this but I must say most of us are under forty years old here so maybe there is some truth in it. When I first heard the chaps in the design office refer to us (in rather disgruntled tones) 'those young Turks in Research' when asked to make something completely new, I thought they were being impolite. But having mentioned this to my more classically educated colleagues I now think it might actually have been a grudging - rather back-handed - compliment. We all work closely with the Design section, because it is Jo (D1) and his team of engineers that design our experimental equipment and the prototypes of the Asdic sets we are working on. We take him the sketches and his designers convert them into working drawings. If it's only a modification to an existing set we usually have a chat and they take it from there.

I often have a drink with Jo down at the pub. It has taken me some time to work out that his name is not actually Jo, but those are his initials. Just as Bob Gamble is not actually Bob. It's similar to school nicknames. That or, in house, we call each other by our surname. Jo is quite a bit older than me, short with a beard and I'm tall and gangly with (they tell me) a young face, so we make an odd pair. But he has an eye for the girls. So we have that in common. And as we both enjoy playing practical jokes I tell him about the first one of mine that backfired.

18. Discovering Chemistry: South Africa, 1930

S.S. *Themosticles*

Our holiday over, Mom and I bade goodbye to Dolly Knapp and left Australia on the SS *Themosticles*. It was a White Star Line ship the same line that she and I first travelled on to England in 1923. But by this time we could afford First Class. It was good fun because the Australian women's hockey team were on board and they turned out to be thoroughly good sports. While Mom was playing Bridge they took me under their wing and played games with me on deck and spoiled me outrageously. The team had a grand 'Farewell *Themosticles*' dinner before we reached Durban and I kept the menu and their autographs as a memento.

We moved straight back into the flat on Marine Parade with Dad. Our friends the Morrisons had sold their stud farm near Johannesburg and moved to Beech Villas, a flat on Snell Parade not far from us, with their sons Ernie and Lenny. It was above a chemist shop and my parents played cards there on a regular basis. At weekends we and the Morrisons and a big group of friends all went out together. Sometimes we would sail round the island in Durban Bay, then fish and stop off on the island. The women spread out the tablecloths for our picnic lunch on the large flat rocks. The men laid out the rugs and drank and smoked whilst we children climbed on the rocks and generally messed about in the rock pools. Then after lunch the men and we older boys took one of the smaller boats and fished some more until we all returned to Durban.

One of these occasions is etched in my memory. We were in the small boat and the men were fishing when Prof, one of Dad's friends, said to me, 'Eric, do you see that rust on the side of the boat? It shows there's the chemical element iron there'. 'But iron is a metal', I said, 'why is it called a chemical element?' The professor explained, 'A base metal like iron is a chemical element because it only contains one type of particle. Particles like these are called atoms and iron is an element because it only contains iron atoms'. I asked Prof what that had to do with the rust on the side of the boat. 'All metals corrode,' he said, 'except gold and silver. Corrosion is the reaction with oxygen from the atmosphere. This iron' he said, as he tapped a rusty patch on the boat, 'has corroded which has resulted in the rust you see there.' I had no idea it was that complicated and said so.

'And, do you know,' he continued, 'that every element has a symbol which is a code so you can identify it? For iron the symbol is *Fe*, from the Latin name for it, *Ferrum.*' I pointed to a dark grey patch of metal that had been used to repair the side of the boat and asked what it was. 'That is a piece of lead. *Plumbum* is the Latin name for it. It is a metallic element that does not corrode in water so that is why it is used to repair the boat. The symbol for the element *Plumbum* is *Pb*. You may be interested to learn that the elements are set out in a chart called the Periodic Table of the Elements'.

I remember asking him for some other symbols of elements. For example I learnt that *Zn* is zinc and *Cu* is copper. 'But although metals occupy most of the Periodic Table there are some non-metallic elements too,' he went on. 'For example, some are gases. *N* stands for nitrogen gas and *O* stands for oxygen.' I thought it was all very interesting and asked him many questions all of which he answered. I was hooked. The very next day I went straight to the library and looked up the Periodic Table of the Elements and copied it out. Then I learnt it because it was fascinating. At that time I liked the idea of being able to give everything I saw a code.

Not long afterwards, Dad, whilst playing poker with his chums, explained that I was interested in chemistry. The chemist from Snell Parade, Mr. Hedges, was there too and said that I could help him in the shop if I wanted. He would pay me pocket money and instruct me as much as he was able. But I would have to stay in the back because I was actually too young (I was 13 or so at the time) to work in a chemist shop.

I was delighted and went there every Saturday. Mr. Hedges was a very nice man and allowed me to prepare some of the prescriptions. It was the job of the chemist to check that the prescription the doctor made out was correct. If the mixture the doctor prescribed was unsafe then the chemist had to change it. For example, if a bottle of medicine which included the poisonous chemical element arsenic (*As*) had the solids sinking to the bottom then - when the patient had the last dose - it could kill him. So the chemist had to adjust the mixture so the solids did not separate.

I loved working in that shop, measuring out the amounts, putting the jars away in their proper places, finding out what the different elements were. After I had been working there for three months Mr. Hedges presented me with a large tome. 'Here you are, Eric,' he said, 'This is for you. It is my old edition. I hope you enjoy reading it and using it. It is called the *British Pharmacopoeia*. It has all the elements listed in it and lots of other interesting information.' I was absolutely thrilled with it and kept it on the table beside my bed.

Mr. Hedges also let me have various chemicals that I needed for little experiments of my own. That was how I got the anhydrous copper (Cu) sulphate (SO_4) powder for the trick I wanted to try out. Copper sulphate crystals are blue. If they are heated up the water in them is evaporated off and they become an anhydrous white powder. Anhydrous means a substance that contains no water. But if water is added to the powder it turns blue again. That is the magical side of chemistry which excited me then and excites me still.

For my trick I wanted to produce a bubbling blue mixture. So I decided that if I combined Liver Salts with anhydrous copper sulphate powder and then added a liquid I should get a lovely blue bubbling bowlful. We always had Liver Salts — a mixture containing sodium bicarbonate and citric acid - at home because Dad would put a teaspoonful in a glass, fill it with water and drink it while it fizzed to aid his indigestion. Bicarbonate of soda is what Mom used to make her cakes rise. It was going to be such a good joke. And I knew just who to try it out on.

THE PERIODIC TABLE

I	II	III	IV	V	VI	VII	VIII	O
1 H								2 He
3 Li	4 Be	5 B	6 C	7 N	8 O	9 F		10 Ne
11 Na	12 Mg	13 Al	14 Si	15 P	16 S	17 Cl		18 A
19 K	20 Ca	21 Sc	22 Ti	23 V	24 Cr	25 Mn	26 Fe 27 Co 28 Ni	
29 Cu	30 Zn	31 Ga	32 Ge	33 As	34 Se	35 Br		36 Kr
37 Rb	38 Sr	39 Y	40 Zr	41 Nb	42 Mo	43 Ma	44 Ru 45 Rh 46 Pd	
47 Ag	48 Cd	49 In	50 Sn	51 Sb	52 Te	53 I		54 Xe
55 Cs	56 Ba	57 La	58 Ce 59 Pr 60 Nd 61 Il		62 Sm 63 Eu 64 Gd 65 Tb			
66 Dy 67 Ho 68 Er 69 Tm	70 Yb 71 Lu	72 Hf	73 Ta	74 W	75 Re	76 Os 77 Ir 78 Pt		
79 Au	80 Hg	81 Tl	82 Pb	83 Bi	84 Po	85		86 Rn
87	88 Ra	89 Ac	90 Th	91 Pa	92 U			

Dad was away at a race meeting so Mom's friend Dolly Knapp was coming to stay. She had returned from Australia and was missing her daughter who still lived there and I thought a joke would cheer her up. Whilst she and Mom were out shopping I took the chamber pot from under her bed. In it I placed some Liver Salts and copper sulphate powder and put it back under her bed. I thought she was unlikely to notice because the salts and powder were white, the same colour as the china.

I was in a state of (barely) controlled expectation when I went to bed wondering what might happen in the night and if my trick would work. It soon became clear: in the middle of the night I was woken by a terrible scream. It took me only a minute to remember what I had done so I did not get up. Then I heard Dolly open her door. She was still screaming. I heard Mom asking her what the matter was. Dolly said she put on her lamp and got up to spend a penny in the pot and afterwards, when she stood up, there were horrid blue fizzy bubbles in it. And it gave her the most terrible shock. I could not come out of my bedroom because I was laughing so much that the tears were running down my cheeks. It was difficult not to laugh out loud. I could vividly imagine Dolly peeing on the pot and then all those big blue bubbles frothing up under her bottom! I thought Dolly would find it funny because I certainly did. But then Mom yelled, 'Eric', and burst into my room and told me I had scared Dolly nearly to death and that I was in deep disgrace.

As may be imagined the next day I was severely punished. My *pharmacopeia* was confiscated, my pocket money stopped and I was given chores of the most miserable kind. My sympathy for Dolly evaporated after that as I decided that she must have left her sense of humour behind in Australia along with her daughter. But even after being punished I still thought it was a splendid joke and my enjoyment of chemistry was undiminished.

19. Q Attachment:
Scotland, July – September 1942

Postcard of Rosneath, Gareloch and Rhu Point.

Not only have the German U-boats been sinking far too many of our ships in the Atlantic but our convoys taking essential supplies to Russia are under constant threat from giant German battlecruisers. However, the Americans are starting to make a real difference due to their ship building programme. Only in America could they manage such an enormous output. True, the country is large, it is rich and it is fortunate not to be troubled by bombing and lack of supplies. But their sheer industriousness and 'can do' attitude is impressive. Somehow they have managed to galvanize industry into the massive ship construction that we so badly need.

William-Powlett has been over there to demonstrate our new Type 144 Asdic set to the U.S. Navy. Apparently they are interested but not yet convinced. They want to be kept up-to-date with the trials and are watching and waiting. And they are particularly interested in the new attachments we're working on. The first we call the 'Q' Attachment. What the U.S. Navy, the Admiralty and the RAF in particular have in common is the need to detect and destroy U-boats. In spite of some detection success, U-boats are still a huge threat as they hunt the convoys in the Atlantic or lie in wait in the Norwegian fjords ready to come out and attack the Allied convoys. If a U-boat bent on attacking a convoy is detected then the escorts go in pursuit. A U-boat prefers to travel on the surface as it can do so at speed but it often has to submerge to avoid Radar or being torpedoed. It is aware that within a hundred yards of the ship our equipment will not be able to pinpoint it. This is where our 'Q' attachment and the new recorders will come in.

The attachment is a horizontal strip oscillator that, although it will not be able to search as far in front of the ship as the beam created by the main 144 set, will be able to search deeper and so keep close contact with the sub. By tilting the oscillator it will direct the beam (shaped like a thin vertical fan this time) downwards so that at greater depths (750 feet) it can keep close contact at short range (down to 200 yards).

It will use the same dome as the main Asdic set - although I am working on an adaption with a better window - and the same hoist and other equipment. It will have its own driver and receiver and also its own power supply. The projector used is also a piezo-electric oscillator but I have designed this one to operate at a higher frequency (38 ½ kc/s) to avoid interference from the main set's projector. It is still a quartz-steel sandwich type but instead of a vertical 15 inch circular quartz and steel plate design it is made up in long slim rectangular strips.

The design of the quartz sections has taken months of concentrated work to perfect. The components are cut and polished in Bath and sent up to Fairlie. Each quartz-steel oscillator strip is 12 inches long by 1¾ inches square and they are arranged and connected electrically in parallel. To ensure that this is done with great precision, small holes are bored through the steel plates so that they can be connected absolutely spot on to the central plate that is the electrode for both. Then the entire array is encased in a rubber sleeve to ensure it is quite watertight. I get so absorbed in it all that sometimes I have to make myself take a break. I consider taking a trip down to see my mother and telephone her. She tells me how upset she is to hear of the death of Prince George, Duke of Kent. Killed in action. She says he was a glamorous character and that it is a very sad loss. I say that good men are being shot down every day but she replies, "But Eric, it is not every day that a brother of a king dies in a flying accident". Her interest reverting back to commoners, she also tells me that Pam, the daughter of her old friend Eileen Scott, is over in this country nursing. And that Pam needs to get away from the stress of it all.

She persuades me to invite her up here, so I do, mostly to appease my mother but hopefully to get that break I need too. I promise to show Pam a bit of Scotland but with transport the way it is we will have to do it on foot so it will be a very small bit. I meet her at the train station and after leaving her togs with Mrs. Hutton (who has agreed to put her up. For a fee of course, nothing if not canny these Scots) we pack sandwiches and set off. It's a sunny day and one doesn't waste a sunny day in Scotland.

We walk past the tower - all that remains of Fairlie Castle – up Glaisdale Burn to Glensdale Burn and then work our way northwards, towards Kilbirnie and finally down towards Kelburn Castle where the first Commando assault course was based. The ground is uneven and stony but the sky is clear and blue. As we climb the water from the burn takes on the colour of the peat and we both think of the brown stained streams that flow from Table Mountain. The hills around here are quite beautiful covered as they are in heather and the views across the water to the Isles is very picturesque. It seems so incongruous when Pam tells me about the terrible injuries she has seen and how she has had to harden up. But of course I can tell her nothing about what I do.

The MacKays have invited us to have Sunday lunch with them, so I gratefully accept. Spence and Eleanor have two children, Moira and Michael, and I must say I am very taken with them. Children simply say what they think which is very refreshing and amusing. Michael likes to sit on my lap while I show him simple conjuring tricks. Because I make him laugh and he makes me laugh, they laugh too, so we always have a jolly good time when I go there. Later, Pam and I reminisce about the greenness of the Cape landscape, and commiserate about the weather, but we have nothing else in common. I'm not sure if my mother was hoping we'd hit it off or not but there's certainly no spark there. All the same, it is nice to chat to someone from home and remember our life of plenty. But on Sunday night, when I wave her off on her train back, I return to my billet with no regrets for leaving it all behind.

Next morning it is back to work as usual. George, Alex and myself are working as we did with the paper problem. Alex jokes that George and myself have the jammiest job because we are experimenting with the crystals in the lab whilst he is out taking measurements in the bowels of SS *Icewhale*. Or doing tests on HMS *Dunvegan* permanently moored here at Fairlie Pier. I point out that I brave the elements too when I go out on HMS *Kingfisher* to oversee the sea trials we are doing on the prototype of the 144 'Q' Attachment. But what I don't say is that I find going out on the corvette for trials exciting: over to Campbeltown on Kintyre, and maybe further to Islay, out in the fresh air observing and problem solving in my head as we go.

Lately, whilst I am having to concentrate on the production side of things, the experience I gained as a student at the Dunlop Rubber Company in Durban is proving invaluable as I guide George and Alex in our researching alternatives. Rubber has always been used to encase the oscillators. It has to be both pliable and strong but there continues to be a problem with the material deteriorating underwater. Unfortunately supplies of natural rubber are proving unreliable – we used to get it from Malaya - and so we are having to research synthetic alternatives. Dunlop has also had problems getting supplies for their tyres so are very good and help by coming up with products that they think will be feasible solutions. Samples of their suggestions are then tested and trialled rigorously by us.

However, most of them to date are not suitable for long periods underwater, whilst others are not malleable enough. But we carry on whilst still working on the oscillators. Percy Jones is the technician in charge of the oscillator labs. I don't think he is as old as he looks, it is probably his receding hairline that gives that impression. A regular in *Supersonics* productions, he is actually quite a jovial chap. In the lab he has had two men and three girls working on the ideas we come up with but since conscription we have been able to recruit more women. Now that Percy has six girls there we can have a proper production line. Jo Davis is pleased because we can assemble the strips here as opposed to in Bath. It does mean that testing can be speeded up and changes made much more quickly.

But I have to keep a very close eye on the quality of their work. And it frustrates me enormously if it is not done to the highest standard. For example, as far as the oscillators are concerned, it is very important to get the polarity of the sections correct or nothing will happen. The elements are in layers: steel /quartz (positive) steel /quartz (negative) steel /quartz (negative) steel /quartz (positive) and so on. Each of the wafers of quartz and metal plates must be aligned exactly. They are assembled here with a layer of adhesive between the metal plates and the quartz.

It is the strength of this bond and the exacting standards of manufacture and assembly that means that cavitation (vibration) and reverberation does not pose a problem with achieving detection. But, if the girls put a metal plate in the wrong way then the whole thing has to be changed. They have to be taken apart, the adhesive removed, the plates and quartz left completely clean. This must all be done with great care. We can't afford to waste the quartz. It's the best, from Brazil, very expensive and in awfully short supply. Then they have to be re-assembled. Correctly!

Because this quartz is in such demand and very difficult to get I am busy further developing designs for magnetostrictive transducers – oscillators - because they can be used successfully in secondary Asdic and do not require the precious Brazilian quartz. There are basically two types of oscillator, the piezoelectric quartz type and the magnetostrictive one. The former convert electrical energy into mechanical energy the latter convert the energy in a magnetic field into mechanical energy – kinetic energy, the energy of motion - or *vice versa*.

Magnetostrictive transducers use a magnetizing coil of wire wrapped around plates of magnetostrictive material all of which are bonded to and enclosed in, a liquid filled magnetic case. When an electrical current is passed through the coil of wire a magnetic field is created causing the magnetostrictive plates to oscillate. This type of transducer is easier to produce than piezoelectric quartz oscillators and is quite effective in secondary Asdic sets – ones that may be fitted on coastal craft for instance - when highly sensitive recordings are required but at a relatively low level of frequency and therefore accuracy.

I work until late in the lab but here in the summer, with the days lighter for longer, I feel more buoyant although when I stumble home to find only a glass of milk and a sandwich left out for me I long for something more inspiring. How I miss - as well as meat - the more exotic fruits and vegetables. Here, rhubarb (crumble is a favourite) and plums there are plenty of, as well as apples come autumn, and the Scottish raspberries are surprisingly good. But vegetables on the whole are pretty mundane. It all keeps body and soul together but I would welcome some more interesting and nutrient rich meals. Not only for the pleasure of it but also to feed my brain which at times feels as if it should burst.

For much of the time we are working in our own little world here and tend to think that we are battling alone in a vacuum against the enemy. But we then hear reports that the convoys are beginning to have a real effect on curbing U-boat attacks. Smith is sceptical. He is so upset that his Mortar is being dropped for the Hedgehog that he in turn has upset the top brass. However, there are now over sixty Hedgehogs fitted to craft and fitting to anti-submarine escorts has recently started which does give the rest of us hope.

When some RAF officers visiting here from the Marine Aircraft Experimental Establishment at Helensburgh & Rhu talk of the great improvement in their Radar and what it means to operations we recognise that elsewhere there are other Establishments like ours fighting their own battles for technical supremacy and we are reminded of the common, over-riding need to win.

Pam Scott in her uniform

H.M.A/S.E.E. Internal Report No. 96; August 1942 (Unclassified)
E.A. Alexander: *'Sensitivity and directional characteristics of magnetostriction listening units Types 140 and 140X'.*

20. KMS *Tirpitz*: August, 1942

Photograph of KMS *Tirpitz*

The German battleship, KMS *Bismark,* sank the British battlecruiser, HMS *Hood*, in May 1941. At that time *Bismark* was the largest ship of her class and, along with their cruiser, *Prinz Eugen*, it inflicted terrible damage on our fleet. Even though *Bismark* has now been sunk, what happened to our fleet will never be forgotten. *Scharnhorst* and *Gneisenau*, the leading German battlecruisers of their class, also inflicted serious damage to our ships in 1940 and early '41. The RAF then bombed *Scharnhorst* with some success. As a result she spent time being repaired in Brest and as everyone knows only got back to Germany by dashing through the English Channel in February this year.

However, *Scharnhorst* was mine damaged en route and according to reconnaissance is still in repair. That leaves the largest remaining German battleship, *Tirpitz,* posing a threat to the Arctic Convoys from her lair in the fjords of Norway. After losing *Bismark,* and with *Scharnhorst* out of action, the Germans are at pains to protect *Tirpitz.* The Allies suspect that she may not be allowed out in the open sea to hunt but the thought of her lying there in wait, ready at any time to come out and inflict the same sort of damage on our convoys as *Bismark* did, is too terrible for the nation to consider. Mr. Churchill, the RAF, the Royal Navy and the Admiralty are all equally determined that she must be sunk. At the very least, put totally out of action.

In April this year the RAF tried to bomb her. Unfortunately, on each occasion the weather was against them and the Germans put up such a good smoke screen it wasn't a success. Following that, in the summer *Tirpitz* and two other battleships left port and our merchant ships - unprotected by a convoy - scattered. As a result many of our ships were sunk by U-boats. It was a disaster. *Tirpitz* then returned to Norway and holed up in one of the narrowest fjords, surrounded by mountains, too far from our air bases for Britain to attack. We are all aware that she is lying there in wait, like a great smouldering dragon. She is dangerously close to the route of our Arctic Convoys that are taking urgent wartime supplies and armaments to our allies in Russia.

Royal Navy destroyers that escort the convoys of merchant ships carrying these vital supplies are stationed up here in Scotland on Loch Ewe and when they leave here they have one of the worst missions of the war at sea. Their ships can be literally lifted out of the water in the tremendous gales that batter them in the Arctic Ocean. They are at times unable to walk the decks due to the huge build-up of ice and the freezing temperatures can cause their equipment to stop functioning. And should crew go overboard in these horrific weather conditions they will most certainly perish.

The last thing Arctic conveys and their escorts need is *Tirpitz* on their tail. Valuable resources are being wasted protecting all of our fleet with escorts and watching the fjords just in case she comes out to attack. We need to sink her but destroying her is not as easy as one would think. By all accounts she is very well camouflaged and highly protected. Impossible to get at her from the land and almost as difficult to attack by air. That only leaves access to her from the sea. Obviously, to sink her, the first hurdle will be to get close enough without being detected.

It's well known that the early warning measures the Germans have in place are a problem. For example, we know that they have anti-submarine nets lying across the mouths of the fjords to protect their ships and submarines from our vessels. With their shore batteries ready to fire at anything and everything, patrol boats constantly covering the fjord and floodlighting at the entrance, overt attack is nigh on impossible. In spite of all this our war lords have apparently been putting in a great deal of effort working out how to sink her for a very long time now.

The narrow twisting fjords that enemy ships hide in are impossible for conventional submarines to navigate. But at Fairlie we know that the Royal Navy, and most probably other establishments, are now working on midget craft that could theoretically get right into such fjords undetected. These are the human torpedoes and miniature submersible craft. The Chariot is a craft that has two divers riding on a torpedo but, as it does not have much range, it is more suited to espionage in port. The one or two man submersible craft, however, like the Welman, are more suitable and should be able to reach the target.

Nevertheless, to do so the chosen craft will have to find its way through the anti-submarine nets. These hang below the water but will probably not reach the sea bed. The craft will therefore have to cut through the nets or go under them to get into the fjord. From aerial reconnaissance we know that _Tirpitz_ is also surrounded by heavy protective anti-torpedo nets. They will be very difficult to cut. But as it is not likely that these will reach the sea bed – we have been advised that these probably only extend about fifty feet down - the craft could theoretically go under them.

To go under them is not as easy as it sounds however. The submersible will have very poor visibility underwater and if contact with the anti-torpedo net is made the craft will be detected by the battleship's hydrophones. Nevertheless, assuming the craft safely negotiates both nets, mines or explosive charges could be placed under the battlecruiser and set to detonate later. The submersible could then (hopefully) make quick an escape before detonation. Although by this time in the operation detection will be less of a worry.

Here, at Fairlie, we first knew something was in the pipeline some time ago when we started work on something so secret (classified 'Top Secret', highest priority) that we were only given half the picture. It is like a jigsaw, those who are working on part of the puzzle do not know what those on another part of the puzzle are trying to solve. Security, of course.

Those of us scientists working on anti-submarine detection devices have been asked to develop an Asdic suitable for such a craft in record time. One that is capable of detecting the anti-submarine and anti-torpedo nets as well as the ocean floor and the target. This is to aid the passage of the submersible craft under or through the nets to reach the target. It is a task that does not promise to be easy.

21. Australia: 1929 - 1930

The Sidney bridge nearing completion, 1929

In 1929 the journey to Australia took four weeks. Mom and I left Durban for our holiday in the height of summer, December, so expected the weather to be good but in the Indian Ocean it was rough at first. Not long after we left South Africa the crew caught an albatross on board. It was raffled and a man on the Captain's table won it. I was surprised to find what a beautiful bird it was with its completely white head and breast, slanting slit like eyes and large orange beak curving to the tip. I helped measure its enormous grey wings which were twelve feet from tip to tip. What a span. It was so large they had to let it go very soon after they caught it.

I was a curious lad and enjoyed helping the crew whenever I could. I was fascinated when they started to erect a canvas swimming pool on the deck and it was also great fun helping them empty the thing and refill it with seawater. Even our baths were filled with sea water. But it was not warm enough to swim in a pool for a lot of the voyage and so everyone did physical exercises on the boat deck instead. This was especially the case when the ship turned south to the Antarctic and we were warned that there would be danger of icebergs until we turned towards Tasmania and Australia.

That stage of the journey I found particularly enjoyable and would go up on the top deck and look out for icebergs. After the first time I did so I took the precaution of wearing my mackintosh and hat because there were albatrosses circling overhead. They would glide, circling around on the wind currents until they fell asleep then, when one least expected it, they suddenly let rip and an enormous blast of white pooh landed all over the deck. …and anyone on it! And if the albatrosses didn't get me then the seagulls did.

And we did see icebergs. From the ship's library I had gleaned that only a tenth of an iceberg's volume was visible out of the water leaving nine tenths of it under the water. Thinking about it I understood what a risk that was and how easily a ship could collide with that unknown underwater mass if they were not keeping a good watch. With stories of the sinking of the *Titanic* in my head I made sure I was up there whilst the alert was on – a memory that was to haunt me fifteen years later – in the inflated hope that I could somehow help avert it. Or at least be in a position to get in a lifeboat.

Fortunately we reached Fremantle safely, visited Perth, refuelled in Adelaide, sailed towards Tasmania and finally disembarked in Sydney where we met Mom's friend Dolly Knapp. Dolly took us everywhere including going over on the ferry to Manly Beach across the harbour on the south shore. It was fascinating to see the steel bridge they were building across the harbour to join the north and south shore of the city. In an enormous arc shape it was the most unusual bridge I had seen.

When it was finished pedestrians would be able to walk from the city over to Manly Beach. Cars would be able to drive across and it was even designed to take trams and trains. As yet unfinished it looked like an enormous pair of pinchers – much as it would look when it opened to let ships through – but at that time it had gigantic cables holding up the two halves. When it was near to completion the cables would be removed and the two halves would join up, making it the tallest structure in Sydney.

Dolly Knapp loved to recount stories about it: she said a very old man working on the bridge fell in the water (Mom said he was probably squiffy) and was eaten by sharks. Apparently it had happened more than once. That peaked my rather gruesome boyish interest and I took a snap of the bridge. For years afterwards whenever I saw that snap I remembered the snap of the shark's jaws. We did get to see a shark at close quarters. Not very far from the bridge was Taronga Zoological Park which had seal ponds and a huge new aquarium where they were keeping a Great Blue Shark. Dolly Knapp said that the shark was very sick for some time but that one day it burped and a man's leg came out. I had no idea of the truth of that story but I repeated it to everyone - still do – as it never fails to make the listener gasp.

Mom wanted to visit another friend in Melbourne so we left Sydney by train to go over the Murray River to the border with Victoria. When we got there we had to get out and board another train to take us to Melbourne. The trains in the state of New South Wales (Sydney) were a different gauge to those in the state of Victoria (Melbourne). They used the Standard Gauge in NSW where the distance between the rails was 4 feet 8 ½ inches. Interestingly, apparently it is the same distance that there was between the wheels of Roman chariots. But in Victoria they used the Broad Gauge, which was 5 feet 3 inches wide.

Mom could not get over how ridiculous it was that one lot of trains didn't fit on the other tracks. A gentleman in our carriage overheard her and told us that not only were there different size gauges between states but that were even different size gauges in the same state. In Victoria they also used the Narrow Gauge which was 3 feet 6 inches between rails and an even much smaller size gauge still which was only 2 feet 6 inches. This was for the tiny little steam trains that took goods and people up to inaccessible places like the farms and forests around

Melbourne. It was quite confusing, he said, and it was later quite a lesson to me in the importance of standard measurements for efficiency.

We had arranged for my parent's friend, Ted Adams, to meet us at Flinders Street Station in Melbourne but he couldn't find us at first – it was incredibly busy - because he said he was looking for a lady with a small boy and I was much taller than my mother by then. After fortifying us with tea he took us to meet his mother and sister with whom he lived in a house on the Yarra River. Painted white with high ceilings and a tin roof, it was very similar to the houses in Durban.

The Adams family organized an oyster party in our honour and I helped make the punch. The adults drank and played cards all evening and it was the morning after that party that Ted Adams taught me how to make a Prairie Oyster – he knew I enjoyed making the punch - which has probably been the most useful recipe I have ever known. I have it still: *2 teaspoonfuls of Worcester Sauce; 2 teaspoonfuls of Brandy; 1 teaspoonful of Vinegar; 1 teaspoonful of Tomato Ketchup. Mix well, drop the yolk of a fresh egg in the glass, and add red pepper on top. Drink down in one.*

It was also after that party that Mom said that we should not take advantage of Mr. Adams' kindness any longer and should find somewhere to live. I overheard in a conversation with Dolly sometime later that she 'did not want his attention'. Mom heard that fashionable new apartments had been built at St Kilda's, a very British area with 'lots of life'. We took a flat on the third floor of a block on the St. Kilda's Road near to Albert Park from which we could see a lake from our balcony. Travelling into Melbourne soon afterwards we watched men erecting the most amazing model of the Cenotaph in London – all constructed out of cardboard – for the Anzac Day parade. It was enormous and so lifelike. I watched as the men unloaded it from open lorries and, balancing precariously on ladders, built it up. We didn't actually see the parade because we were out of town but I was terribly disappointed when we went there soon afterwards and found it had all been dismantled.

The bonus for me living in St. Kilda's was that the flat was not too far from a splendid amusement park called Luna Park. The entrance to it was spectacular: a pair of towers with the giant face of a man called Mr. Moon in between. To get into the park one had to walk right through his huge smiling mouth. I took no interest in such things as the carousels - although the dodgems were fun – but I was enthralled by the Big Dipper. It was a very high roller coaster that ran up and over Mr. Moon gate with further highs and lows all around the park like a scenic railway. Everyone sat in roofless carts which went increasingly faster as they travelled up and down the track before finally slowing to a stop. It was only years later that I appreciated how much I had gained from that trip to Australia, how I used ideas I had come across in my later practical work - images would involuntarily be conjured up - and how that roller coaster ride was my first lesson in kinetics.

Mrs. Alexander, Eric and friends, 1930

A roller coaster is designed using the physics of work and energy. The roller coaster chain performs *work* to pull the cart uphill to its highest point. The cart thus acquires gravitational potential *energy* – the energy of vertical position - which is at its greatest at the top of the hill. The cart then accelerates as it coasts downhill and the gravitational potential energy is converted into *kinetic energy*, the energy that an object has as a result of its motion.

The cart of the roller coaster has reached its greatest kinetic energy when it is at the bottom of the hill. The cart will then coast up the next climb and the kinetic energy is converted back to gravitational potential energy before it coasts down the next hill. At the end of the ride, when the cart coasts to the end of the track, the energy has almost dissipated and the cart comes to a stop.

22. Midget Submarines: Scotland, October – December 1942

Photograph of a Midget Submarine

At last I get a night off. I'm invited to a farewell dinner for the William-Powletts. Myself, Paul Vig and the Astburys go up there together. The house at Fairlie Burn was requisitioned as the Navy Mess from James Tennant. It's a fine place with a decent reception room and a lovely panelled dining room. My mother would be impressed as she always appreciated a smart dining room and a well laid table.

Evening dress is required – mess dress for officers, dinner jackets for civilians - and fortunately mine is still holding up. When the trousers get too shiny I don't know what I'll do. Can't afford to waste coupons. I probably won't even be able to get a pair second hand. Every local body up here is shorter than me and anyway it seems that all the unworn dinner jackets and trousers have been cut up. The women have been re-fashioning them into civvy suits. Tennant's daughter, Laura Boyle, now acts as hostess for most of the dinner parties held at Fairlie Burn.

Whenever any top brass are here - or officers visiting from any of the services - then that's an excuse, in Laura's eyes, for a dinner party. More often than not, if it's not too hush hush, she is sure to have invited some single women. Laura's a nice woman, homely, must be at least fifty. But, like a lot of women that age, she rather fancies herself as a matchmaker. Her children are grown but not quite old enough to be tying the knot. It is probably fun and helps keep her busy whilst her husband is off on duty and certainly none of us take it seriously and are happy to have female company.

Sure enough I am seated next to a very pretty girl called Poppy. I have met her before; lovely smile, dark hair, good figure. She was a clerical assistant down at Portland then came up here with the Establishment. Vig introduced her to me. But she has been going out with another chap and I have been happily biding my time. A friend of hers, Pat Pavey, is seated on the other side of me, but she spends the evening concentrating on what Nordtvedt, one of the Norwegian officers, has to say. And I get to concentrate on Poppy and jolly good fun she is too.

So we have a very merry farewell supper for Newton and Barbara. He says he is relishing being back on active duty again but sad to be leaving such a vibrant establishment. We all say, 'Hear, hear,' because that's what is expected. But when Barbara says she is very sorry to be leaving us we could tell she means it from the heart. Says she is lucky to have the children to keep her busy. She doesn't say: to stop her worrying. A supportive service wife to the core.

It must be much easier, less worrying, to be single in war time. Much more fun anyway. We certainly prove that when Nordtvedt and I walk Pat and Poppy back to Fairlie. There are no street lights and no-one is allowed a torch so we rather stumble our way home. In warmer weather we sometimes take our jackets off if there's a crowd of us so we can at least see where each other is by the whiteness of our shirts, or we follow the glow-worms in the hedges. Poppy and Pat are staying with a friend and we have one heck of a time finding the house. What with quite a bit of drink, the odd pee behind a hedge, and one thing and another, we have a very silly and unstable journey. On the strength of which we make a date to go out somewhere together the next weekend.

When everyone hears on the news the next night about Montgomery's victory over Rommel at El Alamein we are all buoyed up. At last a British victory – perhaps the tide has turned. Then, at the Establishment, out of the blue, Smith is gone. Just like that. There is a mixed reaction. I know he was causing a bit of a stir but I'm sorry because he was an honest chap who could see possibilities in things. He liked simple solutions which always appealed to me. He was also very decent when I came up here. No-one seems to remember that it was he who was instrumental in the first design of strip oscillators after the last war.

However, within two weeks, we have a new Chief Scientist, Dr John Roberts. Australian, works at Cambridge. Since joining the Admiralty mine-sweeping has been his particular area so I think that may have an influence on my oscillator work. I have already been looking into Asdics that will improve mine detection. We also have a new Captain A/S.E.E., Peter Cazalet, to replace William-Powlett.

Yes, it is all happening here. A couple of miles up the coast in Largs is the Hollywood Hotel. It has been taken over so many times that I have trouble keeping track of it. Set up earlier this year as HMS *Monck* it is now HMS *Warren*, Headquarters Combined Training (CT) for senior officers' overseas assault courses and that sort of thing, and for the 'Combined Operations' for all three services. Meanwhile, part of Combined Training Centre (CTC), RAF *Vanduara*, is based at the Vanduara Hotel. It is the two-storey building situated at the north end of the grassed area of Largs sea front, nearly opposite Barfields, the theatre, where I have trodden the boards.

Although nearly all of the hotels have been taken over by the

Admiralty and Royal Navy (not to mention Army and Air Force personnel) it has all been so seamlessly accomplished and change of use so completely absorbed that to the outsider the town still looks every inch a seaside resort with its guest houses and hotels. Of course, the whole of the west of Scotland is a prohibited area to those who do not have legitimate access. To prove their credentials those who live or work here have passport like small green identity cards with their photograph and passes are required to visit places out of the way. At the same time, miles away in the Isles and the Highlands, other large properties house secret Establishments and training bases that no-one has any idea of. It's a marvel of organization and subterfuge.

Norman Astbury goes from here to such a secret location to assess the prototypes of the latest midget submarine. In trials at Loch Cairnbawn (known by security as Port HHZ) the small Welman, built by the Army, is not delivering as it should. The Admiralty are pretty convinced that it is not up to the *Tirpitz* job. Astbury says that the fact that there is no periscope - to do reconnaissance without surfacing - is part of the reason. The vision without it is very poor. Not to mention that there is no room for a diver, so no net cutting possible either. In addition, mines would have to be released from inside the craft.

We are still working with the Welman submersible in mind for other future operations but there is a possibility that our special Asdic set will be used in a larger midget submarine, capable of getting under *Tirpitz'* nets. These craft have been designed and developed by the Royal Navy, prototypes of which were ready for trialing this spring. Although they are still small they can carry out everything a full sized submarine can.

They are designed for three crew (the diver was a bit of an afterthought) but, although larger than the Welman, they should still be small enough to get under the nets and up the narrow fjords to the target without being detected. But they cannot travel at the speed of a large submarine and will not be man enough to get to the fjords under their own steam. Even a full sized submerged submarine would take several days. They will obviously have to be towed to within a few miles.

When they have been towed far enough, some way from the fjords I expect, they will make way under their own steam until they encounter the anti-submarine nets. The midget submarine will have small viewing ports but once it has dived vision will be poor. One of the crew will be a diver who will have to cut a way through the nets with a hand held hydraulic cutter. But the heavy anti-torpedo nets are another matter.

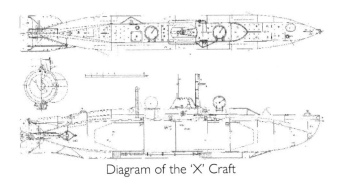

Diagram of the 'X' Craft

An Asdic set will be needed that, first, can pick up echoes from the net at very close range, and, second, can perform at a frequency too high to be detected by the target. The Asdic will ping on the net – if my design is up to it - then move down its surface slowly, ping, ping, pinging as it goes. When there is no longer an echo it is at the bottom of the net, it can then slip under it, go forward, and rise again to reach the target. The craft will carry mines that can be attached to the hull of the target ship or another Asdic set I am refining - an inverted echo-sounder - will determine when the craft is directly beneath the target and able to release charges (attached to each side of the craft) on the seabed below the battleship.

I have been so tied up in it all I have quite forgotten about my mother. When Poppy asks about her I realise that I haven't been down to see her for quite a while. In a burst of filial duty I phone her and she tells me that there have been fewer and fewer night raids and none at all these last weeks. As a result she has felt more confident and is going to evening performances at the theatre again. This means she can spend afternoons at the cinema instead. But it is the radio that is her constant companion (she never misses Tommy Handley's programme, ITMA) and playing Bridge is her constant source of mental stimulation. I notice the slight sighs but refuse to respond, deciding that my mother is having her own fun and is bearing up perfectly well without me.

There is little time for visits anyway because it is round the clock in the research labs and offices at the moment. We all have our noses to the grindstone with regard to our own particular area of expertise but we are still involved with everything everyone else does too, to a greater of lesser extent. Bill Jackson has been working on Plan Position Indicators (PPIs). Ben Browne has been involved too, as has Tom Emerson, Vig and myself. We have been working together on one for the midget Asdic set.

PPI's are scanning systems that pick up echoes of mines or submarines and display them as an image on a cathode ray screen. It is a similar Radar display to that used in aircraft. The target appears on the screen like a small dot or pip. The distance this is from the centre of the screen shows the range — the distance — of the target from the ship or sub. Whenever I work on them I have an involuntary memory of my little Brownie camera and my fist photographs.

Because the pips are shown in real time on the cathode ray screen and are therefore not visible for long the only way to store the information is to take a photograph of the screen. PPI's were first devised in Britain but before the war an American developed a refined version of the cathode ray tube that was able to store the image for long enough for it to be photographed.

I don't spend much time socially with Browne who, as he's single, lives up at Fairlie Burn. He works mostly with the oceanographer, George Deacon, so I don't see them on a daily basis. Browne lectured at Cambridge on geophysics, a specialist area which is useful to us. We all of us work closely with Tom Fry and Joe Fisher who are both brilliant mathematicians. Joe is also a medical doctor, an amazing chap. Lives with his wife Ethel in a bungalow up at Noddlesdale Burn near Largs. They have an absolutely fascinating collection of jade. If any of us need detailed theoretical calculations or mathematical formula, it's Fry and Fisher we turn to. I have never seen men who can use sliderules as fast as they can; Fisher has an amazing cylindrical one like the Tower of Pisa nearly two feet long. Jackson is married and keeps himself to himself but Emerson is a chap with a bit of fun and he enjoys the amateur dramatics. And I think Vig, Willis, Fisher and myself get on so well because we share a similar sense of humour.

Then two bits of news at Christmas. Smith has been appointed Director of Scientific Research at BAD in Washington. I'm pleased because although he ranted a bit he didn't deserve to be humiliated. A good post like that with the Admiralty should help to heal his wounds. Also, all women are to be conscripted. What this will mean to hundreds of families around the country I don't know, but the women I speak to in the Largs shops all tell me that they can't wait to get out and do their bit. Anything to escape the boredom of housework. They don't know yet how repetitive the production line can be. They will need to make the most of time with their families this Christmas. Not sure yet where mine will be.

H.M.A/S.E.E. Internal Report No.106; October 1942 (Unclassified)
E.A. Alexander: *'Polar recording camera for directional curves'.*

H.M.A/S.E.E. Internal Report No.108; November 1942 (Unclassified)
E.A. Alexander: *'Directional properties of A/S 334 and 364 magnetostriction assemblies'.*

H.M.A/S.E.E. Research Note No.1; December 1942 (Unclassified)
E.A. Alexander: *'The directional properties and power measurements of A/S 299 Double-rubber-covered oscillators'.*

23. 'X' Craft:
Scotland, January – March 1943

Photograph of 'X' Craft towing training

We are hoping for some good news for a change. It's true that losses to U-boats are still very high and the North Sea routes are still in constant danger from attack - an average of over 130 ships lost per month during 1942 has been cited by our Captain - but with Hedgehog's improved hit rates, our refined anti-submarine detection equipment, the recent improvement in RAF Radar and the massive output of American ships, we are praying against all odds that we may be able counteract the losses and turn the tide in the North Atlantic at the least.

In mid-January we learn that there has been an uprising in the Warsaw Ghetto. Both young and old Jewish inhabitants are forced to work in German manufacturing factories but still, in spite of being hungry and cold, manage to rebel against yet further deportations to camps like Treblinka. Incredible courage but to no effect I am afraid. Where will it lead, I wonder, and fear the worst. Britain and the U.S.A. have vowed to be avenged of these abominations but there is nothing our troops can do now to stop them. It could become quite depressing but the amount of work we have to get through is a very good antidote to letting it engulf us.

The first clear weekend there is, when the snow has finally melted and I can see the snowdrop heads nod in the banks along the roadside, Poppy and I cycle down to West Kilbride to see Moshe Feldenkrais and his wife, Yona. We hope we can lift his spirits after yet further news of the horrendous Jewish persecution. George Deacon and his wife, Margaret, live close by, so join us for tea and pancakes, or blinis as Moshe insists on calling them. He is a real character and a thoroughly amusing chap. A refugee physicist and engineer who often works with Deacon. I don't work with him myself but we have long chats at lunchtime because he is someone who is interested in so many different things.

One thing he is keen on is co-ordination and fitness, and he is passionate about a form of meditation to control bodily functions. He has observed how children move and thinks we should do so as naturally as them. I too believe in mind over body so we have lively discussions especially as we share a rather corny sense of humour making puns: he agrees with me that the canteen food is a bit bland; I say lack of ginger could be the root of the problem; he says ginger would certainly spice things up. That sort of thing.

Anyway, we are digging into the delicious tea and all getting along like a house on fire when Moshe's wife (a doctor at the local hospital) receives a telephone call to say there is an emergency and can she come and help. We imagine some awful accident and take our leave quickly with as little fuss as possible. The next day he tells us that it was a small boy who had his head stuck in a saucepan. He was playing soldiers and wearing it like a tin hat and could not get it off. Apparently a good greasing with Vaseline helped lubrication and finally did the trick. As it does for so many things.

We hear that the giant German battleship, *Scharnhorst*, is in Altenfjord in north Norway, threatening (like *Tirpitz*) to attack the convoys travelling to Russia. Then we are informed that Chariots - essentially one-man torpedoes - were transported to Norway to mine the *Tirpitz* whilst she was anchored up. Everyone here was quite surprised that such a thing had been attempted and, understandably, knew nothing whatsoever about it.

Unfortunately, due to choppy waters the attempt was abortive and one charioteer was lost. What happened to the others we have not been told. The Chariots are not up to such a task but we already assumed that. Land, do a quick job, and get away is about their limit. We believe this is why the Admiralty and the Navy are pushing the submersibles more than ever.

George has dragged me into joining amateur dramatics again and he's talked his girlfriend, Rita Dawson, (a clever mathematician, working on sound drift) into it too. He, on the other hand, keeps out of the limelight. He's very keen on the production side, says he's not pretty enough to be an actor (his excuse is that he wears spectacles) but I think he's a bit shy. Somehow, I've been cast as a toff. Have to wear a monocle, smoking jacket and cravat. Poppy says I really look the part. Fortunately, though, not many words again. I think they've worked out that I'm not a natural.

Poppy, and her friends Pat and Nan Gurney, are all cast in the play as well as Percy Johnson and Tom Fry and it turns out to be very good fun. After the show we have a cracking party. Some of us, including me, keep our costumes on and I must say being in a costume makes one act quite out of character. I was gallant, polite, charming and urbane. Until I perhaps had one or two too many cocktails then I reverted to type. Poppy said I flirted, told awful puns, made suggestive comments and danced with every woman there. Sounds like the real me. I think she must have gone home whilst I was trying to do the limbo with Ethel, Joe Fisher's wife.

A chap from the Medical Research Council is up here trying to find out the physiological basis of Asdic operation. Vig and Deacon are helping him with it and even Law and Dawson are providing information. The Admiralty are still trying to perfect recruitment of Asdic operators but finding that too many applicants are failing the aural and intelligence tests. I think the renewed interest in operators is because the final prototype of the Top Secret miniature submarine, 'X' Craft, has been delivered from Vickers to Helensburgh and sailed over to Port Bannantyne, the new base for midget subs. They will be used as training craft, hence 'XT'. Designed originally for three persons the hatch has now been adapted for a diver but there is no more internal space. The diver will have to squeeze in with the Commander, the pilot and the steersman. The entire craft is now approximately 50 feet in length, with a hull diameter of approximately five feet, but there is a great deal to fit in there.

After ongoing trials, we accept that to cover all eventualities with the nets a diver will definitely be needed on board any submersible craft used to sink the *Tirpitz*. This is plainly not an option with the Welman but it will still be very difficult in any other submersible. The diver will have to get into his rubber diving suit, flood the chamber, open the hatch, climb out, cut the anti-submarine nets strand by strand with a net cutting gun. He will then have to make sure that the propeller and rudder of the craft do not become entangled in the loose strands it as it goes through the opening. Finally he will have to re-join the craft. All this could take many hours. It will be heavy, laborious and freezing work. It will also be enormously risky although it should be physically possible.

Then, after cutting through the anti-submarine nets at the opening to the fjord, the craft will have to breach the thick steel mesh of the torpedo nets protecting the *Tirpitz*. These will be too heavy to be cut and the craft will have to go under them. We have been informed that these probably only hang down about 50 feet in the water. Even if they hang lower they will not reach the sea bed. Because Willis has already been involved with HDA and midget submersibles – and is working on another HDA set to use in small craft - he co-ordinates our research.

After much experimentation I come up with an Asdic set that can work at close range using a quartz oscillator that can get an echo from these thick metal net constructions. The craft will need the Asdic to guide them down the net because vision from the submersible is virtually nil. A small cathode ray oscillograph will provide an easily read display thanks to Jackson et al.

We are still re-arranging the oscillator and training shaft for use in the 'X' Craft. In place of oscillators constructed of cylindrical plates I am working on square wafers of quartz piezoelectric crystals that have a frequency well above the hydrophone listening devices used in any battlecruiser. They will be built in strip form so that several can be arrayed in a very compact way. To ensure they are watertight they will be completely covered in two-ply rubber or, if testing results remain inconclusive, then the most superior synthetic rubber we have and on which Alex and George are working.

Tests and trials are underway constantly. In tandem, we work on one echo-sounder to determine the depth of the water below the keel (Type 151S) and thence the ocean floor and one up-turned echo-sounder attached to the conning tower to measure her distance from the net above (Type 151). As well as the Asdic set to find her path down the net and the path ahead. In conjunction these – in simple terms - will indicate when the 'X' Craft is under the net, find its path to the target and the same upturned echo sounder will indicate when it is directly beneath the hull of the battlecruiser but above the ocean floor enough to deposit its charges on the sea bed.

There is still so much to decide and perfect and, needless to say, the utmost secrecy surrounds our work. Degaussing also has to be carried out. The chance of using the 'X' Craft before the days became too long is now in doubt. Despatch of the *Tirpitz* may have to wait. Overall, the design of the equipment has taken all our ingenuity and undergone arduous testing but in our trials the set has done very well. We are all pleased, myself, Willis, Norwood, Jackson, all of us. But each one of us feels it is a tremendous responsibility.

The Asdic set (Type 144) that we are trialing on HMS *Kingfisher* will be introduced shortly and should make quite a difference tracking U-boats. It will also be suitable for fitting in minesweepers. Production has also started on the 'Q' attachment. At the same time as we have been working on the oscillators for the new 147 Sword (used for determining the dept of the target). This new set is completely independent of the main set and the 'Q' attachment, although it does work in conjunction with it. It is not housed in a dome but has a streamlined electrically tilted 'sword' which contains a piezo-electric oscillator 18 inches long. As thin as a blade it has a wide horizontal beam, operating at 60 Kc/s and the oscillator is completely encased in rubber. The design has not been easy to achieve.

The depth determining Asdic is designed with a new ahead thrown weapon called the Squid in mind. Squid is a long range depth-charge thrower designed to throw its charges ahead of the ship or submarine it is attacking that we have been working with for some time now. The explosives go further, more reliably and more accurately, and sink faster than those from the Hedgehog.

Training the ratings is ongoing. Amongst the most novel training aid in my mind are the mobile attack teachers which are converted buses. They contain Asdic sets capable of simulating a real life attack situation. I can just imagine the ratings when, returning from convoy duty, they see a red London double decker bus draw up at their base only to find that it is not a jolly outing but a baptism of fire. On the bus they will be put through their paces and tested to their limit on the Asdic sets.

Roberts and Jock Anderson (one of the original scientists from Portland) are both supplying the more usual mock Asdic apparatus used for training purposes in attack table exercises to the Admiralty in Queens Square. In the mock-up an imaginary submarine tries to escape from the Asdic operator who is in his imaginary ship. The big wigs can hear the Asdic echoes during the exercise and may come to understand pitch discrimination and assess reverberation. A follow-on from the Medical Research I think. But it has got to be easier to grasp in a large well-proportioned room than in a cramped bus. Although a cramped bus is probably closer to real working conditions.

Obviously the Admiralty want to be sure they have the very best operators but men who are good Asdic operators are born not made, the training officers tell me. They say that those with a good ear, like musicians, or even linguists, have an innate ability to differentiate between echo pitch. An experienced man can usually tell the difference between a submarine echo and an echo from a wreck or a large rock formation.

A whale or even a large shoal of fish can confuse an inexperienced officer into thinking it is a submarine. Whales in particular can be a problem, especially killer whales, and not for the obvious reason. If a whale is frightened, it may stay submerged for up to half an hour. A sleeping whale or a basking shark is also motionless, not unlike a drifting vessel. Their outlines appearing very similar to that of a submerged submarine. Likewise, a wreck on the ocean bed. So it is not a straightforward task for the men we rely on to pinpoint the German subs before they torpedo us.

Eric as a toff in a monocle in a *Supersonics* production

Work at the moment is so pressurised that I feel the need to clear my head in order to come up with solutions. A very brisk walk down to the harbour after lunch gives me not only a bit of exercise but lots of fresh air to awaken the brain and clear my mind, ready for the next session. If the fishermen are still about – perhaps mending nets or working on their boats - I stop and chat. And very often they sell me half a dozen herrings that they wrap in newspaper. It has happened so often that now I keep an oilskin bag in my overcoat pocket to carry them in. If I am lucky Mrs. Hutton might cook them in oatmeal for my breakfast. And as I make my way back to the Establishment that sea salt smell conjures up my South African childhood.

H.M.A/S.E.E. Internal Report No.116; January 1943 (Unclassified)
E.A. Alexander: 'Directional characteristics of Staybright domes, A/S 15, A/S 300 and A/S 162X'.

H.M.A/S.E.E. Research Note No.4; February 1943 (Unclassified)
E.A. Alexander: 'Asdic repeater'.

H.M.A/S.E.E. Internal Report No.117; February 1943 (Unclassified)
E.A. Alexander: 'Quartz steel oscillators as frequency standards'.

H.M.A/S.E.E. Research Note No.15; March 1943 (Unclassified)
E.A. Alexander: 'The directional characteristics of cylindrical perspex dome casings'.

24. Cold Waters of the Cape: South Africa, 1928

Eric at the mouth of the Amanzimtoti River

Whales and dolphins, crayfish, squid and shoals of sardines. So much part of my childhood in South Africa, still very much part of my work in Scotland. I remember with pleasure that there were always huge shoals of sardines when we went to Amanzimtoti in July, mid-winter, a little way down the coast from Durban. Sardines only swim in cold water and when the storms and tides pushed the cold water towards the Cape coast the sardines got swept along too.

The shoals would stay as deep as possible in the day to remain out of reach of predators. Then they came up to the surface to feed in the evening when they sensed it was safer. However, at any time of day there were also plenty of gannets ready to swoop down, dive straight under the surface and spear sardines with those deadly sharp pointed beaks of theirs. It was the dolphins that alerted the gannets that the sardines were coming.

Dolphins follow the sardine shoals and whilst doing so they were always great fun to watch. One might push its long snout out of the water, followed by another one then another one. Before one knew it there would be a whole shoal of them. They seemed to have a sense of fun, enjoying swimming together, jumping and playing games with each other. The glossy black and steely blue colours of their coats like the colours on the inside of a conch shell. Their colour, shape and movement designed better by nature than anything man could achieve. And their extraordinary and complex means of communication something that I was to eventually emulate in my chosen career.

In May, autumn time, there was an absolute plague of sardines. The water was stuffed with them. There were so many sardines washed up on the East Cape coast at Umkomaas that they could be caught in buckets. It was known as the sardine run, their annual migration. All the locals from the village would be down at the water edge. A great crowd of men and women shouting and laughing, pushing and shoving to get some sardines. Even little children, black bottoms and raggedy tops, picking them up and putting them in the tins their big brothers and sisters held out. Plenty enough for everyone.

The fishermen would lay out their nets end to end near the water's edge. Then lift the long line of nets bulging with hundreds and thousands of little silver sardines flipping and jumping and curling their tails up. These were simply emptied into large barrels - it must have been the easiest catch they had all year. In the evening everywhere there would be the smell of wood smoke and sardines grilling. Whether it was the hobos on the beach, the locals in the villages or us in our yards, everyone had old tin cans sawn in half and filled with charcoal on which to cook the sardines.

We and our friends would set a tin on a low stone wall and stand there turning our sticks of sardines, careless of any that dropped onto the ground. Sardines so plentiful that nobody cared to lose a few. The dogs would wait with wagging tails and tongues hanging out, more than happy to clear up any tit bits. Eating self-caught sardines, sitting on the stoep, candles alight in old jam jars, nothing could have been better. Served with half a lemon to squeeze over and fresh sliced bread and butter and with big fat pumpkin fritters covered in sugar and cinnamon to follow, it was a meal fit for a king.

When my parents and I visited Cape Town, which we did every Christmas time throughout my childhood, we would often go for a spin with our friends to Muizenberg. From the top road there we looked down over False Bay and wondered at the length of the beach and width of the bay. Further on, at Simons Town, my father and I would pick out the ships that belonged to the Royal Navy where even today some of our troops are stationed. I wonder if they too do as we did and walk past the fishing boats tied up along the harbour side and buy fish to take back for supper.

Looking down on Muizenberg beach

It is well known that whales come to breed in False Bay in springtime – which was why there were whaling stations there - as well as along the coast at Hermanus where they like the warmer sea that the Angulas Current brings down the coast from the Indian Ocean. But Humpback whales also breed in the same warm water of the Indian Ocean eastwards along the coast near Amamzimtoti where, if one is in luck, they can also be spotted.

However, whales can also be seen there in August, in the middle of winter. One might be watching the dolphins and the gannets and all of a sudden notice a mound, perhaps a big wave or something afloat in the water, then suddenly the realization dawns that it may be a whale. A great big brooder whale might push its huge jaws out of the water, go back under and as a finale smack the water with its tail. It thrilled me as a boy and made me want to find out more about the whale but, even today, when I understand the science and how a whale can impact on under water detection work, I still find it the most awesome sight.

At Seapoint in Cape Town, on the coast of the Atlantic Ocean far from the Indian Ocean, the water is freezing so suited to other species. When I was a child we sometimes stayed with my mother's friend, Beattie, in her flat there. Close by was a strip of sand and a stony beach with rocks but only a masochist – or a Scot - would swim there. My favourite outing with her was to picnic on those rocks where she liked to catch crayfish for us.

There are ledges under the rocks along that coast formed from the constant movement of the sea over thousands of years and the crayfish would cling under the ledges, between the rocks, where the water flowed in and out, washing over them. It was necessary to lie down on ones stomach and put ones hands under the ledge and pick them off. Although sometimes they would be tantalizingly out of reach.

Lion's Head from Seapoint, Cape Town

Beattie was small and thin. She would lie on the edge of the rocks and two of her house staff would take her by the ankles and lower her down so that she could get her arm down between the rocks and grab the crayfish that were hard to get. When I was about nine – and before

I grew taller than everyone else – she let me catch them which was the highlight of my holiday. Then a fire would be lit and the crayfish boiled in old four gallon tins on the beach. We ate them as soon as they were cooked, warm and succulent, tasting of the sea. The flavour has only been bettered since by those I have eaten here, on the harbour side in Scotland.

25. Squid: Scotland, April – June 1943

Eric, Pat, Nan, Nordtvedt & Poppy

The heather covered moors of Scotland remind me of the *fynbos* clothed hills of the Cape, in many ways. It is the lack of trees, flowers, space and wide open skies. And there is no doubt that the islands of Scotland are quite beautiful. Walking up the hill sides, looking down over the Clyde, or the lochs like Loch Striven, raising one's eyes to the islands beyond it is a truly majestic sight, as my mother would say. But the sunset over the Isle of Arran is so spectacular that it beats everything else hands down.

Needing a break, the six of us - Nan and Engelsen, Pat, Nordtvedt, myself and Poppy - take the ferry from Largs over to Arran. It is still chilly in April but we climb up Goat Fell, the mountain that dominates the island. The jagged peaks are all that remains of the rim of a volcano. Geologically Arran is very interesting as in the past it was thought that the coastal rock formations of the island — which unusually has two different types - could hold the clue that the earth is older than we have previously thought.

The wildlife of the island is also rich: golden eagles, gannets and herons, seals and otters, as well as the dreaded midge, all flourish in the unspoilt landscape and the wonderful views from the peaks are unrivalled. Engelsen takes a snap of us all then Nan does, although I suspect it is only a picture of her Norwegian she wants. Bluebells are out in the woods which the girls go into raptures about — after the winters here I have some sympathy — and I must say, having never seen such a thing until I came to Britain, it is a sight to be marvelled at. And the promise of summer and warm weather that the flowers bring is very welcome. They underline the pleasure we feel to get a weekend off and the chance to re-charge the batteries.

This year has been so busy, as busy as ever I suppose. In America trials of our Asdic set, Type 144Q - comprising range recorder, bearing recorder with automatic training and the 'Q' attachment to search deeper — have gone well. The U.S. Naval Research Laboratory (NRL) have had it for quite a while and we gather they are impressed with the improved tracking. Production has therefore begun immediately. Just wait until they see what else we have.

Research in other areas also continues. The acoustic torpedoes recently deployed by German U-boats are having a much more devastating effect on our ships than our ship's passive torpedoes have on them. Currently a U-boat is detected by the Asdic set on one of our ships by the echoes it receives back from it. The Captain of the ship gives the order to fire a passive torpedo that will travel in a straight line towards the direction of the U-boat. But once the U-boat knows it has been detected it will, given enough time, get out of the line of fire by changing direction or escape by diving deep.

U-boats - vastly outnumbering our escorts - are hunting in wolf packs in the Atlantic whilst lone hunting U-boats are fitted with acoustic torpedoes which are more devastating in their ability to find their target. This means that if one of our ships becomes aware of a U-boat close by and tries to take avoiding action the U-boat's acoustic torpedo will continue to follow the course of the ship by means of the oscillator fitted in it. The ship will be hit, possibly sunk. It is very difficult for a vessel to escape a hit by a torpedo that is homed in on it.

To date these U-boats are finding our ships before we find them but as soon as our convoys of merchant ships and corvette escorts learn to move together to increase their chance of detecting and deterring U-boats so they increasingly deploy the larger and faster frigate on the convoy to go on the attack when U-boats track them down. The combination of this tactic alongside more exact Asdic detection, better Hedgehog hit rates and improved Radar in airplanes – especially if there is an aircraft carrier included in the escort – should mean there will be a greater chance of counteracting the wolf pack threat.

Here at the Establishment, Jackson has been investigating acoustic torpedoes for some time, with input from myself and others. In particular I have been heavily involved developing an aerial launched new echo-controlled homing torpedo model. It uses two active quartz oscillators in the nose with the active speed of it below 20 knots but it is all still in the very early stages.

A while ago we decided to hand over some of our torpedo research but we are all of us so pushed on other more pressing fronts that something more has to give. At our most recent regular meeting we unfortunately come to the conclusion that with such an enormous amount of investigative research still to be done regarding aerial launched acoustic torpedo in particular, and with all the other more pressing demands on our stretched resources (mostly time), we will not be able to come up with anything in time to help the war effort. So, regretfully, we at Fairlie and the powers that be at the Admiralty have decided to shelve further research for the time being.

Our research data therefore goes to the U.S. and Jackson will pass it all over to the Americans. They have the resources and time to develop the aerial acoustic torpedo and already have research facilities and underwater sound laboratories dealing with their own homing weapons. However, I am particularly interested in torpedo technology and as the Admiralty will continue to research and develop wire-guided torpedo have, with an eye to the future, told both Vig and Law that torpedo research is definitely something I would like to develop further after this war is over.

To remind me of all we have achieved so far I have held on to the model of the prototype homing torpedo designed to be launched from an aircraft. With its elegant shaped, heavy metal body, retractable fins and ring tail it makes an interesting sculpture on my desk and acts as a very useful paperweight.

In the meantime, I am required to make the journey down to the Admiralty in London nearly every month now. I take the train and if I am very lucky sometimes catch a less-than-red bus across London. I walk up Whitehall to Admiralty Arch and on into the Admiralty – all dark shiny wood and polished brass – where I give my progress reports to the powers that be seated around an enormous table, some I have got to know, others I meet for the first time and some of whom are occasionally also from the Establishment.

They grill me about every aspect of underwater acoustics including hydrophone, Asdic development and the new dome for the 'Q' I am working on and I answer their many questions. I have brought the notes I am expected to make on all aspects of Asdic equipment and operation and any suggestions I think pertinent and, after being dismissed, leave these with the secretaries there – one of them will type up my reports and arrange for them to be circulated to any craft that may benefit – and escape back outside into the real world of bomb sites and devastation before returning again to the rarefied and serene one of the Establishment.

Whilst we have been testing the 'Q' attachment our colleagues have been studying the new, improved, ahead-thrown weapon, Squid. There is no doubt that the deployment of Hedgehog has made a tremendous difference to U-boats kills with far fewer of our ships sunk. However, this long-range depth-charge thrower is different from the Hedgehog in that it will be automatically operated and controlled by the new depth determining Asdic set we are designing, Type 147. The Asdic will set the depth on the Squid fuses electrically, whilst the Asdic range recorder fires the mortars automatically. The three-barrelled mortar, like the Hedgehog, discharges its projectiles ahead of the ship.

However, Squid projectiles – small bombs similar in weight to the Hedgehog depth charges – explode when they reach their depth setting which produces a great improvement on the rate of kills. Overall, the advantages over the depth charges fired by the Hedgehog is that, first, the fuse is of a type that is set automatically to the accurate required depth. Second, they have an improved sinking speed and reliable under-water course. Third, the projectiles are fired whilst still in contact with the U-boat eliminating 'blind time'.

Another benefit of the Squid is that the mortar design has reduced the size of the recoil forces which means that it can be fitted onto smaller craft. We do mock-ups of most new gear as ship fitting is an expensive job (money and more importantly time-wise) and we do need to know that it is working before fitting is undertaken. Squid gear might be rigged up on deck for example and the crew take it through its paces. Usually a Commander and an engineer (and sometimes a scientist like myself too) go along on the trial. It often throws up a snag or two and this can be corrected before the gear is rolled out.

We have changed the 147 set to operate at a frequency of 50 K/cs so I have refined the original design of the two ply quartz-steel oscillator so that the strip is 18 inches long and 1 ¾ inches square, completely covered as usual with the thickest synthetic rubber we have. The array is now tilted at 45 degrees backwards in the vertical plane and it can be adjusted to allow the depth of a U-boat to be determined from point of contact until the projectile is fired. It is all encased in a metal housing with a Staybright window.

I've been on various tests and trials regarding this new Asdic and Squid, the last for six days. At Oban we observe the corvettes waiting to escort the convoys and, feeling thoroughly in touch with the action, it is brought home to me how our work could save the lives of all those who sail on them. On several of these occasions I see Catalina flying boats land which brings back vivid memories of Durban. From Oban we go onto Tobermoray on Mull so that we can get into the really deep water channels of the Atlantic to thoroughly put the equipment through its paces.

Asdic beams are 'bent' when there are cold underwater currents and this is something we test out in these deep waters. U-boats take advantage of this and they simply sink to great depth and remain there, eluding our current equipment when under attack. Urgency is key in wartime and in May the Admiralty confirms that the tests done on the depth determining Asdic set (Type 147) and the 'Q' Attachment have been very promising and that on the strength of them immediate production of the prototypes is underway. The sea trials of Squid on HMS *Ambuscade*, although not completed, have, to date, been reported as going well. We are all pleased. We are also buoyed up with good news on the military front in May. The fighting in North Africa that started in 1940 with Italy's declaration of war has finally come to an end. The British Eighth Army and U.S. forces have at last been victorious. The AXIS forces have surrendered. What the next move is we don't know but for now morale is high.

Nearer to home, the Royal Navy has formed the 12th Submarine Flotilla at Rothesay for midgets and chariots. Last year Kyles Hydropathic Hotel was requisitioned by the Royal Navy for HMS *Varbel*, the shore base HQ of Twelfth Submarine Flotilla, and it is now used for training crew and operators in the midgets and on the human torpedoes. On my return from trials I glimpse it from aboard ship, up on the hill above Rothesay Bay, looking every inch a crenelated Victorian mansion. No-one would suspect that it is filled with Wrens and Naval officers or that matelots are living in the huts. It is very well chosen because the calm water of Loch Striven to its north is ideal for the sea trials and training on the 'X' Craft.

Astbury and others who have been up to Loch Striven have noted that it is the towing of the midgets craft that is causing the most concern. However, the nights are now too short, the days too long, and with less time to carry out any surprise attack the *Tirpitz* operation will not be possible until the days draw in again. In the meantime facilities for training are much improved, we have time to perfect our equipment and the towing problems have time to be resolved. HMS *Cyclops* is to be the depot ship where most British submariners train and HMS *Bonaventure*, which came up early this year, is now the depot ship for the 'X' Craft. We know the pressure is still on but everything seems better planned and more controlled.

Dering has been up to HMS *Varbel* to see if the latest Asdic equipment is compatible with fitting in the 'X' Craft. Although we are still refining the echo-sounders as their use will be vital to the success of the operation. However, Dering says that the space through which the crew has to enter the craft is very tight. And the space inside is more cramped than an under-stairs cupboard. In fact an under-stairs cubby hole would feel like a castle compared to it.

The men chosen for the operation will be of short stature but the diver in particular will need to be very small and slim. Dering says that even then the diver will still find it difficult to enter and leave the craft, especially with his kit. We have all discussed this at length. Better by far if there is no need to send out a diver at all but use the Asdic to go under the nets.

My mother telephones me in the first week of June. She says she has heard some awful news. Leslie Howard has been killed. His plane was shot down returning to Britain from Portugal. Not even when there were raids on London did she telephone me but news of a film star is serious stuff. 'Isn't it terrible,' she says, 'he was so wonderful in 'The Scarlet Pimpernel' and as Professor Higgins it showed him as the perfect English gentleman.' Rather mischievously I tell her that I have heard the news of his death and that I have some news for her, Moshe says Howard was actually of Jewish blood. Clearly surprised to hear her gentleman actor was not as English as she supposed, but always quick and not one to be outdone with revelations, she replies, 'Obviously, that was why he hated Nazis.' And with that, she says she hopes I am eating properly and rings off.

I am my mother's son and so of course I eat properly. Even in June it is never that hot here in Ayrshire and spring, summer or winter I always have porridge for breakfast. A pinch of salt in it and a little milk on top and that is only to start with. A slice of bacon or a sausage to follow - or best of all a kipper - a slice of toast and a cup of tea and I am set up for the day. Lunch in the canteen is a stew or macaroni cheese but occasionally I take Poppy out to have a treat of lobster freshly taken from the pot. The seafood here is better than in South Africa, now there is something I thought I would never say. I try to remember these things when I speak to my mother next, something to tell her that is not classified. I say she must come up here, I will treat her to lobster. Then she can judge for herself if I am eating properly. 'One day', she says, 'When this war is over'.

Postcard of SS *Duchess of Argyll* at
King's Cross Ferry, Arran

In June, in spite of relatively low losses to U-boat attack, the Admiralty are worried enough about the deep-diving U-boats (in the

North Atlantic they are diving increasingly much deeper than 700 feet to avoid Asdic attacks) that they order Squid even though it has not been fully trialled. Of course the gear can still be modified but it is a clear indication of the desperate state of the war.

26.   The Best of Luck:
Scotland, July – September 1943

Photograph of an 'X' Craft being offloaded

The Allies invade Sicily! We hope that this is another step nearer the end of the war. The road signs have been restored in England so the government have obviously decided that all threat of invasion is over. Up here, however, it continues to be an unfathomable wilderness. Secret training establishments and bases still litter the highlands and islands. Commando courses are set-up not far from here and a new slip has recently been built at Fairlie Pier for landing craft. Well placed for our next secret project.

As we continue to share scientific and technological information with the Americans some of us from the Establishment are to attend the Anti-Submarine Warfare Conference at the Naval Research Labs in the States this month. Law will lead it and concentrate on the review of the depth determining Asdic and the bearing recorder with Hector Willis concentrating on harbour defence, Tom Fry on hydrophones, Rick Dawson, Squid and George Deacon, submarine and mine detection Asdic. That covers most devices. The others of us are rather tied at the moment with high priority tasks.

The Asdic set for the 'X' Craft with my oscillator design is now fully operational. When the anti-submarine and anti-torpedo nets have been located it will give echo-soundings which should enable the craft to travel down the surface of the net, and finally under it, rise again to find the target and release its bombs under the hull of the battleship. Everything should be clear on the cathode ray oscilloscope screen that works with it. But, with the lives of so many men in danger, I cannot stop worrying and go over every detail in my mind day and night. If the craft is unable to get under the nets to the *Tirpitz* then the operation will be a failure.

Apropos of nothing, except we all need a little light relief, we are being treated to an evening of home grown entertainment at the Establishment. All the Departments are invited and if the weather permits it will be held outside, otherwise it will be in the canteen. Moshe is going to give us a demonstration of judo. He teaches it to the ratings up on the mother ship in Holy Loch and has taught some of the lads here. They have all been practicing their moves and Moshe promises us that they will surprise us with their skill. Afterwards Tom Fry's wife - who is a well-known and accomplished cellist - is going to play for us. So that covers the entertainment and cultural side of things. Food is covered by the wives who make a buffet supper with supplies begged and borrowed from everyone and quite a bit wheedled out of our visiting U.S. Naval officers and we have a very sociable evening.

For some relaxation on warm Sundays Poppy and I make up a foursome with Pat and Nordtvedt, take a picnic and, from Burn Foot, climb up Fairlie Burn which falls over several waterfalls into the small wooded valley known as Fairlie Glen. Already the midges are starting to bite - come August they will drive us mad - but I keep telling myself that anything is better than winter when the cold will chill me to the bones. On Fairlie Moor we stop for our picnic and admire the views of the Cumbraes and those on over towards the Isle of Bute.

The girls are doing their best to educate us chaps. I – who never read a literary book for pleasure - am to be introduced to poetry to fill that gap in my education and Nordtvedt is to read it to improve his English vocabulary. Ostensibly. In point of fact I think they are hoping we can show some romantic streak which has clearly not been obvious to date. However, I surprise myself by liking Keats and these sessions do seem to heighten my appreciation for landscape and its effect on the psyche.

We are, after all, surrounded by Scotland in all its beauty, the colours soft, the horizon undulating and the sky wide and cloudless. From our vantage point we also have a wonderful view of the various craft on their way up the Firth of Clyde to Loch Striven. It's quite a moving tableau, not unlike some fascinating medieval water pageant. But the sight of the ships also brings me down to earth - poetry has its place but for me it can never trump practicality.

Earlier this year HMS *Bonaventure* was converted to a depot ship and it has just worked its way up to here with the midget subs on board. It's to be a secret base at Loch Cairnbawn (now known as Port HHZ) for advanced training of crews on the 'X' Craft and Chariots. The prelim trials of the X5 and X10 have gone well and so now attacks and full scale exercises will be carried out involving the capital ships. The crews will have the real thing to work on as the boom surrounding the ships will be fully protected by nets for the crews to try and negotiate. Submarine crews also need to perfect towing the 'X' Craft, which to date has been fraught with problems.

The big war news is that the Polish underground resistance is hoping to liberate Warsaw from years of German occupation and also the possibility of more round-ups. The Germans are now retreating from Poland as the Soviets are advancing. They are winning tank battles elsewhere as our own RAF is winning the battle of the air. Admittedly there have been retaliatory raids in Brighton and now Portsmouth and

London, but they are not like before. It does all seem to be paying off at last. In addition the U-boat threat in the North Atlantic is well down although *Tirpitz* does remain a thorn in the flesh.

Roberts, our Chief Scientist, is due to lead another delegation of British scientists to New York in September. They are due to visit the U.S. Navy Department, the Bureau of Ships and the Naval Research Labs (NRL) who are all interested in what we are doing. It will be a good trip and there is some talk of my accompanying them but George, Alex and I are still working around the clock to finely tune the oscillator gear needed in the fjords and elsewhere. There is simply too much work to do. Too many balls to keep in the air, so we will stay here.

Astbury has now been up to *Varbel II*, the requisitioned lodge that is the secret base at Ardtaraig on Loch Striven, where training on the 'X' Craft for the *Tirpitz* operation has been underway since July. Although this is all top secret stuff the locals cannot but help know some of what goes on. However, they seem to accept that the sea bed explosions, towing and diving exercises and so forth that go on in the loch and along the seaboard are normal naval trials. Then, out of the blue, HMS *Titania* arrives at Port HHZ to act as the depot ship to the submarines that will take part in the operation. There are six subs in total that have all been fitted out with towing equipment especially designed for the 'X' Craft.

My monthly report to the Admiralty in London is as detailed as ever. I sit in the meeting and answer questions about such things as my work on Asdic domes and in particular the one we are adapting for the Q attachment. Then the progress we are making on our depth determining set comes up as U-boats are reported as diving much deeper. They suggest that recorder and depth charge settings should be modified to counter U-boats diving up to 1,200 feet but I point out that this will require more than a simple modification. The Admiralty is clearly worried.

There may be only a few people at the meeting — always if a subject is Most Secret - or there may be many but it is always an interesting and high powered event and, although challenging, it is a welcome chance to take a break from the more creative intensity of the Experimental Establishment I now call home.

London never ceases to enthrall me, even though everyone I meet there seems to have lost their appetite for excitement and it's looking rather battered now. Four years of war - bombs, blackout, queues, food shortages, clothes coupons, beer running out and buses hardly running at all - seems to have sapped everyone's morale. It's even difficult to buy things that some would consider a luxury, others essential. Books are impossible to find for sale (but I can understand this, we have to get our paper for the recorders from America now) and nice soap (stuff that lathers and doesn't smell of carbolic according to my mother) is a positive luxury.

Fortunately, street lights are on again in London and it is wonderful to be able to find ones way around at night without tripping over things or kicking a rat. There seems to be an explosion of them in London. When I open the door of a telephone box to call my mother to say I am in town I am ridiculously thrilled when the little light bulb springs into life. It feels like Christmas has arrived early. I am not sure I ever took any notice of it before.

I decide to make the most of it with a late night trip to Soho for a lively time. There are still hundreds of GI's looking for dance halls or visiting the Rainbow Club on Piccadilly, and where there are GI's, there are girls. But after a couple of drinks in a bar I decide I haven't the stamina for anything else and go to my mother's early, she can always rustle up a tasty meal from next to nothing. She is pleased to see me and is delighted to have someone to spill all her news to.

Hetty has told her that my cousin Sara Miranda, Aunt Rhoda's daughter, has joined the FANY's – the First Aid Nursing Yeomanry - and could be sent anywhere in the world to help rescue the wounded. I don't really remember her as I saw her once when I came to London in 1926 when she was two years old and I was ten. She is now only 19 years old and I think that quite an impressive thing to do but then reason that most of the girls in our Establishment are also that sort of age. Was

I that capable at 19, I ask myself, and have the sudden realization that is what the older men at the Establishment probably think about me. A mere young whippersnapper. After I have caught up on all the news and had a good sleep it's back on the train to Scotland again. It has at least been a break from the relentless work.

Trials and exercises are not easy here in the wilds of Scotland where 'the cold wind doth blow'. The snow has come unusually early this year, covering the mountain sides and moors. Those at Port HHZ feel it physically more than we do here because - apart from the snow - the terrible gales out on the Atlantic mean that the 'X' Craft training exercises are very difficult. At the Establishment it is simply a case that our trials are cancelled altogether. A frustration, nevertheless, because it is something over which we have no control.

In the end it's physicists that make up the delegation to the United States. Roberts is the leader accompanied by Vig and Browne and three others. They sail from Avonmouth and there must have been others from various Establishments. I would be envious if I thought the weather was much better than here but I don't believe it will be. Although, by all accounts, they will do very well in the U.S. with food and drink at a time when we seem to be shorter of everything than ever.

Then a happy surprise – very good news indeed - Italy is out of the war! On the 3rd of September the British Eighth Army and the Canadian troops with those of the American forces effectively liberate Italy from Nazi rule. The Italians capitulate immediately. Prior to this Axis human torpedoes were destroyed having been detected by our Asdic. In addition, after the surrender, a captured Italian escort ship is found to be fitted with German echo-ranging equipment although we are informed that their detector does not have the superior features of our detector sets. Very satisfying to know that our Asdic sets are superior and have really done their bit towards Italy's surrender.

The Germans continue to put up a fight. Whilst they fight on they cannot be fighting elsewhere so we cannot but see that as a good thing. We want them well away from our next planned operation. Astbury has been up at Ardtaraig for quite a lot of the training that has been going on and met some of the Naval divers. He says that although many of them are on the small side they all look sinewy and strong. However, they all tell him it is hell getting in and out of the craft. Nevertheless, after all their training cutting nets they are at their peak – perhaps the delay has been all for the good – and they can now spend several hours working underwater. Even if they do say they think it will freeze their balls off. Not that that may worry them soon.

Those of us at Fairlie in the know are only too aware where they are headed. But the divers themselves don't let anything slip. Both scientists and divers do know, however, that the operation is imminent. Port HHZ is a hive of activity with exercises involving towing submarines and their crews, the 'X' Craft, the recovery gear and, of course, our gear. Finally, the fitting of the charges onto the 'X' Craft is underway and top security measures are in place with all leave for ratings cancelled from 1st September. We are not informed of anything that we do not need to know so are in the dark about certain aspects of Operation SOURCE.

Pat, Poppy and Eric on Fairlie Moor

However, we know all there is to know about the secret gear we have designed and the difficulty of the fitting so feel on absolute tenterhooks. The crew of the 'X' Craft will be the bravest of men because, in spite of what is said, the operation will, quite likely, be a suicide mission. Any one of a number of things could go wrong and the operation fail; the diver might be stranded on the net to find his way as best he can to land, the navigational equipment might err and the craft not find the target, the men left in the craft might get blown up by their own explosives. Brave men indeed. We are all wishing them the very best of luck.

H.M.A/S.E.E. Internal Report No.141; September 1943 (Unclassified)
E.A. Alexander: 'Prediction of performance of Asdic oscillators'.

27. My Box Brownie Camera: South Africa 1927

St Lucia, Zululand

I have always loved water, the stories that revolve around it and the wildlife associated with it. Every year Dad drove to Lake St Lucia for a few days to fish with his pals and he would take me with him. St Lucia is a vast estuary system in the shape of an H. False Bay is a lake that forms one side of the H and St Lucia lake forms the other side of it.

There is no bridge to get over to Lake St Lucia just a small ferry. Only one car – and foot passengers - can go across to the island at a time. Dad would drive the car up the ramp and onto the small wooden pont where a line of youngsters on each side pulled on the cables, guiding them over wheels, until after only a few minutes we reached the other side. Simple mechanical systems such as that pulley fascinated me.

Thousands of years ago the strong ocean winds built up the sand along the coast and behind these long sand dunes lakes and lagoons were formed in the depressions left behind. One of these is the actual Lake St Lucia - about 25 miles long, six miles across but only five foot deep – in which stand three islands. Mangroves grew along the edge of the islands and on their trunks one could see hundreds of little snails, not unlike whelks. At high tide, when the roots were covered in water, the snails would crawl up the trees then, at low tide, they would climb down and nibble away at the roots, eating the decayed matter on them leaving them spotlessly clean.

I loved the sand beach at St Lucia and collected many marine and coral fossils for my museum there. In December and January sea turtles came ashore to lay their eggs in the warmth of the sand and I assume they still do. They would pull themselves out of the sea on their flippers until they got to the dunes. After laying their eggs in the sand they laboriously made their way back to the sea leaving their eggs to take care of themselves.

Behind this around the lakes was a lush landscape, the fig trees hanging with sweet ripe fruit, blue and white agapanthus flowers growing under the trees side by side with vivid orange clivias, bright hibiscus flowers and the scent of frangipani trees filling the air. Beautiful butterflies, some as large as my hand, fluttered over all of this and small birds feasted on the pollen. It looked like I imagined paradise would look.

The lake system at St Lucia is unusual in that it is fed with seawater from the Indian Ocean. The salty sea water is diluted by rain and water from the Mfolozi river but owing to the shallow water evaporating in the hot weather it becomes very saline indeed. Fish thrive in this warm salty water and grow to an enormous size. Of course that was the reason that we went there to fish. Using a small boat we would catch salmon or mullet and sometimes bream. We always caught something for dinner but we never knew what it would be when we felt the pull of the line because it was impossible to see the fish due to the extreme muddiness of the water.

Because there were so many fish in the lakes there were always sea eagles circling overhead. There were also sharks at the estuary mouth and crocodiles at the mouths of the tributary rivers. One had to be vigilant: for example, none of the workers left their little children alone on the shore because a croc could be hiding in the reeds, creep up, steal them away to the water and eat them. There were also many resident hippos. Being herbivores they loved the lush vegetation that grew around the lakes and they made a real racket stomping about at night as they fed. In the day they would lie with their pink mouths wide open while the birds picked their long pointed teeth clean.

They may have appeared peaceful but we took hippos very seriously if we were in the boat. If anyone saw a pair of ears or a nose sticking out of the water we immediately made off in the opposite direction because the hippo could submerge, come under the boat, stand up and lift the boat out of the water. Being in the water with an angry hippo is not safe — they can run extremely fast under water and although they may not eat people, they can seriously injure of even trample one to death.

Not only were there plenty of fish at St Lucia Lake but there were also — or because of it - literally thousands of birds. Apart from the usual ducks, geese, herons and cormorants there were also white or pink backed pelicans bobbing about on the water like beach balls. The most dramatic sight, however, was when flamingos came in great flocks to feed. This stretch of water was many miles long and the flamingos, flying over in a giant V shape, would suddenly land on the water like a vast pink coloured tablecloth. When they all honked it made the most terrible din.

The long legs of the Flamingo make it one of South Africa's largest birds. Their feet are webbed and when they want to feed they move their legs very fast to stir up the mud in the lake. To feed they put their rather strange upside-down beak into the water to find algae and plankton. The bottom of the bill is similar to that of a pelican but, in the case of a flamingo, its main purpose is to keep the top bill afloat. The top bill moves to let algae and plankton into the bill and the water is forced out of the mouth through the filters in the sides, leaving the algae and plankton. After every visit I learned more facts of this kind and they have stayed with me to this day.

I was an inquisitive child and was always directed to the encyclopaedia when I wanted answers to questions about such things as how flamingos fed or hippos got rid of the water in their mouths. This interest in facts about wildlife and in how things worked was the inspiration for my parents to buy me a camera for my tenth birthday. Although it is possible that it was simply something to challenge and occupy me and allow them some peace. How to use the camera certainly took a bit of learning and I had to read and follow the instructions carefully. Loading the film was the first hurdle: one had to pull out the winding key to open the camera and, taking out the roll holder, remove the special paper which protected the spool of film from light.

If the spool was incorrectly loaded the paper would get between the lens and the film so it had to be put in very carefully over the rollers, through the longest slit of the reel and the spool turned to grip the paper. It was a very difficult procedure. When the roll holder was replaced in the outside box it was essential to make sure that the slotted end of the spool was next to the winding key which turned the roll of film.

Having concentrated and achieved loading the film there was the satisfaction that I had accomplished the task and then there was the excitement — for a boy of my age in a mechanical rather than technological age — of turning the key and watching the little round red window. First, it showed a warning hand symbol to take care, then turning further a number 1 would appear indicating that it was ready to take the first snapshot. Many years later I realised that I had learnt more than just how to use the camera. I had also learnt to do things in a measured way and to follow the correct process. Although I appreciated even then that when I made a mistake it was usually because I had taken a short cut.

After some fuzzy snaps I worked out that if I held the camera close to my belly it didn't wobble and cause the snapshots to be blurred. I looked through the finder on top, held my breath and pushed the exposure lever with my thumb until I heard it click. Having taken the shot I had to remember to turn the winding key ready for the second photograph. There were various other refinements — like Stop Openings and ways to change the slides to take snapshots in the shade or ones with lots of sky - but Dad suggested that I concentrated on the basics to begin with. I experimented and mastered all of them over time but they seem complicated now compared to the ease of use of my most recent modern camera.

When the film was finished I took the spool of film out to get it developed at the photographers. Our friend Harry, Dolly's husband, was a photographer and he did it for me. I can remember the excitement of collecting my first snapshots and the pleasure I felt. It is the same feeling I get now when one of my experiments works in the lab.

28. Bullseye:
Scotland, October – December 1943

Photograph of the German battleship *Scharnhorst*

Bullseye! *Tirpitz* has been hit. Not a kill but severely hurt. We have spent the days since the start of Operation SOURCE in a state of tense expectation and worried anticipation. Any one of a number of things could have gone wrong; the submarines towing the craft may have had difficulty; the 'X' Craft diver may not have been able to get in and out of it without mishap; my Asdic may not have picked-up the vertical nets and the echo-sounder may not have been able to determine the depth of the water below them so that the craft could get underneath. Finally, we were very concerned that the echo-sounders were able to guide the craft into position beneath the *Tirpitz* hull so that the saddle charges could be detached.

Fortunately, it would appear that at least some things went to plan. Although details of the Operation are still classified the more senior of us have been informed that the midget subs were towed out to within a few miles of the fiord although not without incident. One or two didn't make it. Tow ropes are blamed. It is infuriating if all this developing, planning and training – not to mention safety of the men – could be put at risk by such a simple component. We may get the full story sometime. However, two or three of the craft were able to make for the nets. Exactly what happened once they were out there on their own we do not know. Nor, I suspect, will the R.N. for quite some time as no men returned. So none of us know how many laid charges or how many charges – which each contain 2 tons of Amatol - were dropped beneath the hull. But we do know from reconnaissance that at least one of them exploded beneath *Tirpitz* and inflicted serious damage.

As for the crews, they always knew and accepted that there was a strong likelihood they would not get back. They were all very brave men and we can only hope that those in the successful craft have somehow made it to the mainland and escaped. That would be the plan. Because it was always understood that there was very little possibility that our 'X' Craft could get out of the fjord again and rendezvous with their towing ship.

The crew were briefed that whatever happened the most secret equipment and paperwork on board had to be destroyed if they were at risk of capture or had to scuttle the craft. Sensitive paperwork such as maps could be burnt, or top secret notes even ingested, but whatever happened the Asdic equipment on board must not fall into enemy hands. The oscillator and cathode ray screen would have to be destroyed and that would be a hammer job. Of course, if the explosives took the 'X' Craft too, then there would definitely be no worry about the Germans getting hold of, or hearing of, our secret equipment.

We still have plans for them for another Top Secret operation. Both Willis – who is working on HDA to locate underwater obstacles - and my team, who are working on Asdic to suit 'X' Craft, are already hard at work. I am also working on Asdic homing devices and a magnetostrictive transducer that will operate at 10Kc/s to facilitate underwater signalling between a parent submarine and small surface craft and one capable of detecting underwater obstacles.

Browne, Deacon and the other oceanographers have been researching oceanic tidal and wave energies for some while now. With the next operation in mind it is crucial that we take everything into account including the weather. Storms as far afield as the Caribbean could create waves and swell that might affect operations on northern shores. If the oceanographers can predict conditions then the best possible time to carry out any operation could be chosen. Or the worst avoided. Nearby, along the coast at Wemyss Bay in Largs, ramps have recently been built and a basin dug out in the entrance to the river so that landing craft training exercises can be undertaken. Combined training is now a regular feature here as personnel from HMS *Monck* have moved into billets close by.

So we all carry on and, as usual, research, refine and improve our gear all the time. A phrase used by Maggie, a friend of my mother's in London, always comes to me when I have to hone some equipment. 'Adopt, Adapt, Improve'. It is a motto apparently and it so perfectly describes our experimental work here at the moment that I have taken it for my own. As there seems to be as much to do as ever I have been lucky enough to get some more staff to help out with oscillator research. Miss Walker, who has a physics degree, joined up first and has been a real help.

Now Mary McKechnie, who was lucky enough to start her English degree before there were restrictions, has been drafted here but her friend, Kathleen, who has joined her has fallen foul of them. She flunked her maths degree but is not allowed to retake it until the war is over as she has been conscripted. I tell her that the practical work will help her but in fact all the girls accept their war effort with good grace.

Our little team takes the latest oscillators onto HMS *Dunvegin* and in rotation the girls take the readings at various frequencies, recording the (vertical) x and (horizontal) y co-ordinates for Alex. They also accompany him out on SS *Icewhale*, our mobile laboratory, to take acoustic measurements when we test the oscillators under sea conditions. The extra hands all help speed things up a bit. And it does mean that when the weather is very rough and the girls get sea-sick down there in the stuffy bowels, there is always another one of them to take over.

On a personal front, Poppy and I have stopped seeing each other. I am happy to carry on but Poppy wants me to make a commitment. She doesn't say it but she means she'd like us to get engaged. But I simply cannot see myself marrying Poppy. Don't know if it's because she is too much of a dolly daydream or simply too nice. I think I'll need someone more challenging. Anyway, I am far too involved with work and I'm just not ready to get married. Put on the spot with no time to come up with a gentle landing, that's what I told her and I'm afraid it went down like a lump of suet. And my social life along with it.

Feeling a little deflated both Willis' and I have decided that we cannot stand the canteen food any longer. It is not that it is bad, it is simply not good. Too stodgy - suet again - and not very appetizing. I suppose we have merely been eating there too long. Marie has suggested we eat at Nan's Café along by the harbour. Nan does the cooking, her mother the serving. We will have to make sure that we don't discuss work but that will be good for us.

Donald Hotchkiss, who was in Willis' office at the time, overheard and has asked if he can join us. He is a dry old goat (he's over fifty and been working on underwater weapons since the Great War) but Marie felt she had to say yes. Never mind, he doesn't stop us having a sociable lunch he just doesn't add to it. So at 12.30 on the dot we walk into the village and get a two course lunch for one and threepence and it's all very nicely served up. Meat and two veg followed by a decent pudding. Not long afterwards the other single chaps suggest we go to the dance hall in Largs. The trouble is that the girls there all want to dance with the service men (including GI's who with their offers of gum and candy set the bar too high) and it is in my opinion too much effort especially as it shuts at 10 o'clock. Fortunately there is still some social life to be had near at hand. A few of us from the labs have been invited to dinner at Fairlie Burn because Stanley Darling, a Royal Australian Naval Volunteer and Captain of HMS *Loch Killin*, is to dine. His frigate is in dock for fitting and they always do themselves proud when there is a visitor. The standard of food is better than usual and there is more alcohol on offer.

I think Darling is very impressed with the house. Vig and Browne let him think that we all live in this handsome building in these salubrious surroundings. He asks where we work and they point out the huts behind it. Laboratories, workshops and design studios, they tell him. Fortunately the other chaps who are billeted here don't enlighten him. He's convinced I'm sure that we're a very quaint, tin-pot operation. Only a little Establishment where some scientists live in a nice country house and work in a few sheds in the grounds. It will be a good ruse if he truly thinks so. We certainly can't let him see where the real powerhouse is. There must be getting on for over two hundred of us now at the Establishment, including all the auxiliary workers.

Anyway, throughout dinner I have some very encouraging conversations with him. He is interested in acoustics - in fact trained as an Asdic operator before coming to Britain - so this is a very good start. His ship is one of the new class of frigate and so would expect to be rigged out with the latest gear. I explain that it would be invaluable if we could use it for trialing the new Asdic oscillator Type 147B (Sword) and 'Q' attachment to see how they perform out in the deep waters at Tobermory. There have been some teething problems with the 'Q' oscillator in trials to date so we need to be sure they have been addressed.

As importantly, others around the table would like to see how Squid performs on it. The *Loch Killin* is in the right place at the right time from our point of view. Fortunately Darling proves very open to our using his vessel and quite likely sees the possibility of securing some of the latest gear for it. I am delighted that when the time comes I shall definitely be on board for a spell. On the strength of which I enjoy the cracking meal of scallops followed by grouse, with extra relish. As it happens, HMS *Hadleigh Castle* didn't get to New York during Roberts' visit, when it should have, but may shortly arrive. The frigate is fitted out with the depth determining Asdic (Type 144), the 'Q' attachment as well as our latest Sword, so the Americans will be able to trial them and monitor their performance for themselves. We have all been waiting and wanting to hear their reactions so it is frustrating. And as Roberts has been on leave since getting back from the U.S. (Jock Anderson has stepped into the breach and taken on his duties) we are a bit up in the air. To be able to use *Loch Killin* is a heaven sent opportunity.

It is so cold here at the moment that I am reminded of my first winter in Oxford and am wearing two vests. I write to my mother to ask if she has seen any of the new-fangled string vests for sale in London. The naval divers here swear by them. She says she will have a go at knitting one. She is struggling herself with the weather down there and says that freezing fog is the worst thing possible. Apart from the awful weather, the occasional damage from a stick of bombs and the resulting looting, the worst thing she thinks it necessary to report is that getting a bottle of Scotch is a matter of great luck and costs an arm and a leg.

The Boyles (whose family seem to own most of Fairlie) have been very kind to me since I have been without a girlfriend, inviting me to dinner and cocktail parties. Laura and Dulcie Boyles' husbands are some sort of distant cousins but Dulcie is widowed. Her husband was a Colonel in the army and was killed at about the time I arrived here. She has two daughters, Grizel and Pam. Dulcie, who works in the drawing office here, is very nice and has taken pity on me. I told her I needed some Christmas cards to send everyone so she has arranged for me to have some printed. *Peace and Happiness*, is the wording inside and it would be wonderful if only that could be true.

Dulcie says she understands it's not easy being single with no wife to do all the social side of things. I have already realised that, on the whole, a single chap is forgiven a lot but I have to do what I can, apart from sending cards, to say thank you for hospitality. I've bought the women handkerchiefs or, rather, my mother has tracked some down. And I have managed to get my mother some perfumed soap for Christmas. She will be very impressed especially as it is in an attractive wrapper. One of our scientists visiting the States bought several bars back and I exchanged one for a bar of chocolate.

Everyone has a whole bar of Cadbury's milk chocolate a week on ration. I limit myself to one square a day which means one square a week is left over. After the first eight weeks of being here I therefore had a spare bar. This has built up to be quite a store and the drawer I keep the chocolate in is nearly full. But it seems we have been taking our rations for granted. At the Establishment we have been told (Top Secret) that there is only enough food left for two, three weeks at most, and that we must improve our detection rates in fast order. The government doesn't want to lose any more food supply vessels. This is meaty stuff, excuse the pun. The powers that be do not want to feed any rumours. They cannot stomach it. I could go on but enough is enough. How we are to achieve such a thing in so short a time I don't know but there will be no Christmas holiday for us.

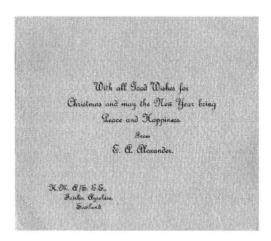

With all Good Wishes for
Christmas and may the New Year bring
Peace and Happiness
From
E. A. Alexander.

H.M. A/S. E.E.,
Fairlie, Ayrshire.
Scotland

Our Captain gives us an uplifting Christmas message that thanks to our improved detection we are sinking more U-boats than they are sinking our ships. The improved Radar fitted in our aircraft has been forcing U-boats to operate submerged and in doing so they have been detected by our more effective Asdic. So pleasing to know that all our hard work is actually getting results. Perhaps we are finally winning the Battle of the Atlantic. Then, on Boxing Day, another Christmas gift out of the blue. The German battlecruiser, *Scharnhorst*, so long a threat to our convoys, is sunk off Norway's North Cape. Well done, Royal Navy. Perhaps we are finally winning this Arctic Campaign too.

H.M.A/S.E.E. Research Note No.33; December 1943 (Unclassified)
E.A. Alexander: *'The effect of a rubber covering on the sensitivity of an Asdic oscillator'*.

29.   Asdic Type 144:
Scotland,   January – March 1944

Photograph of HMS *Hadleigh Castle*

I notice a very pretty new assistant at a drawing board when I pop my head around Willis' door in January to say I can give him some time to talk through his latest project. High cheekbones, freckles, blue eyes. Dark hair and neat figure. I take it all in. Very nice. Marie tells me her name is Muriel McKinnon and that she asked 'Who was that?' when I left. 'Dr. Alexander', says Marie, 'Scientist in charge of Oscillator Research'. 'Well, he's got a bit of a cheek, hasn't he' was her reply. Marie says it was because of the way I calmly stood there and slowly looked her up and down. She says I can give the impression of undressing a girl when I do that. As if I would.

Miss McKinnon comes from Glasgow and, only one year into her degree, has chosen to join the Establishment. She's obviously got a bit of spirit because she's already in the cast of the *Supersonics*. In the next production apparently. With one of her boyfriends. She didn't waste much time. I haven't the time for the amateur dramatics myself anymore. Not that I was any good. These last months have been so frantic.

We are all pleased to hear that HMS *Hadleigh Castle* has finally arrived in New London, Connecticut. Both operational demonstrations (some mechanical and electrical tests included as well as some overside ones) and laboratory tests of ranging and listening Asdic equipment have been carried out. As the main 144 Asdic set uses the 15 inch diameter piezoelectric oscillator that I have been developing as a projector (made up of quartz and steel sandwiched together) I am very pleased that all went well. The quartz crystals in the oscillator are connected in parallel. A heavy steel plate constitutes the negative electrode between two layers of quartz crystal and each one of these in the assembly is rounded to the projector case by flexible connectors.

To eliminate the 'blind spot' caused by the horizontal beam the echo ranging 'Q' attachment is designed to be used in conjunction with the main set and this too was apparently well received. It is designed for ranging and maintaining contact with deep submarines at short ranges. The projector used in the 'Q' attachment is of a totally different shape to the cylindrical ones in the 144. It is a piezo-electric oscillator of course, but it is a strip type 12inches long by 1 ¾ inches square.

The principle is the same as for the Type 144 but is constructed of square sections of steel sandwiched between square sections of quartz. All electrically connected in parallel as before. But in this one there is a central interplate acting as the high-potential electrode. It is even more essential that this smaller oscillator is precision made with not only the components ground to the hundredth of an inch but the adhesive between the quartz and the metal plates must also be completely even. To ensure this thin copper wire is laid on the plates, covered with adhesive and then the quartz wafer. This not only keeps the electrical connection but it ensures that the adhesive between each section is absolutely even and standard and the gap between each layer is exact.

On this side of the world the action is more deadly. In January the RAF carry out a heavy raid on Berlin and the Luftwaffe retaliate with heavy bombing in London. I call my mother and she says that she is alright but it was a very unpleasant surprise. The odd bombs lately were nothing compared to it. Woken in the middle of the night it is the worst raid she can remember, lasting for a couple of hours. She has rather got out of the habit of making for underground and found getting about the next day very difficult as transport and trains were quite disrupted.

My mother says she is bolstering herself for the next round but underlying her stoic exterior she seems very apprehensive. Instead of *whenever* this war ends, she now says, *if ever*. I repeat my offer of accommodation up here in Largs but her social life is obviously still important to her. She asks me what has been on at the local theatre. I tell her there is only one theatre open in Largs and that the Establishment does its own amateur productions. 'I think I am better in a place I know,' she replies immediately.

Then good news from the Eastern Front, the Soviets have finally lifted the siege on Stalingrad. The German 6th Army cut off the city in 1941 and it has remained besieged ever since I have been here in Fairlie. But, awful as it has been for the starving and freezing Russian inhabitants of the city (it is reported that those who did not perish had to eat rats and even sawdust to survive) it turned out to be one of the worst - or best — German military decisions of the war to date. Hitler wasted resources and men that he could have been using against us. Thank goodness. Had he studied those dreaded Napoleonic Wars we may have been in a very different situation today.

The rubber encasing our oscillators continues to be a problem. Sometimes is not up to the job and wears badly, other times the rubber flanges or fittings are not well enough manufactured and therefore not watertight enough. I used to find that when I went to sort out sets that were not working on vessels the constant movement of the set was as much of a problem as anything else. But I think we are improving the standard all round now.

We have been hard at work to find synthetic alternatives to rubber for over a year now. It must be able to remain stable at very low temperatures. All rubbers, even synthetic ones, change when they are subjected to low temperatures such as in the deepest waters of the ocean. They will crystalize and can become brittle. We have tested them all and few of them have come up to the job although now and then we get a breakthrough. Isoprene is an alternative we have tested extensively but it looks like another synthetic polymer with a different chemical structure may be better so we concentrate on developing that.

In February we get the sad news that the light cruiser, HMS *Penelope*, has been torpedoed and sunk off Anzio (where the Allies are fighting the Germans to capture Rome) with the loss of over 400 crew. It always hits the R.N. chaps here very hard and we scientists – saddened to hear the news of course - are nevertheless interested to see what gear was used and if we can learn from it. Indeed, whatever the war news we civvies just carry on as before, more refinements, more modifications. More trials and tests.

Cazalet, Captain of the Establishment, has moved on and our new Captain, R.J.R. Dendy, takes over. He's a pleasant chap. Wife and daughter. Outside of the Establishment people we come across all think it will all end soon but we know that there is still a great deal to do as threats await they can never imagine. Even though I'm pushed, I manage to find time to go in and see Willis or Vig if they send me a message that they would appreciate my input on something or other. We all work in offices on the top floor. Vig, Marie, Hector and Miss McKinnon share one office. George and I share another. The labs and design office are below.

Spence Mackay is in charge of the labs and his - and others – offices are divided off the lab with Gyproc sheeting. The lab itself is very large, approximately 50 feet long, with benches right down the middle. Percy Jones may be in charge of the actual production line for the oscillators but it is Dulcie Boyle who listens to the girls' concerns. She tells me when she thinks I've been too harsh. I don't think I am harsh but it's essential that every component is made exactly to specification. She says it would be preferable if I did not come in and say, 'That one is wrong' or 'That is not in line,' and so on in quite such a peremptory way. Apparently it upsets the girls. But it wastes time if I have to preface everything with an English apology. So I leave Dulcie to mop up the tears on the production line.

Our gear for the forthcoming top secret operation – all to do with the timing of the invasion of France that everybody knows will happen at some time - must be fully developed and operational before the summer. We have the target date, which means, with everything else, we are working flat out. I'm so pressed for time that I have a word with Vig one evening over a pint and ask if he can find me some help. An assistant to help me do calculations would save hours. 'Ask Willis if you can borrow Muriel,' says Vig, 'She has been nagging me to find her some scientific work. Says she didn't join to be drawing or doing clerical work as my PA. I promised her I'd try and honour the agreement. You'll find her quick enough'.

Miss McKinnon has turned up. Says Willis can spare her for a couple of days a week. She is mostly only re-drawing the plans for Hector and Marie's reports anyway, which is a bit of a waste of a brain. I don't need to show her how to use a sliderule because they can't live without them in R&D and she has already mastered the technique. As she can use a sliderule I've asked her to check a whole page of calculations, which she has managed to do much quicker than I expected. It means that I can get on with more important stuff. I must say that a pretty girl perched on a lab stool is more attractive sight than staring at George's pate.

Muriel (I have her permission to drop the title) has a sense of humour, thank goodness, and the day seems to go faster when she's helping. Not that she stands any nonsense, mind you, makes very disparaging faces if she thinks I've been a bit cheeky. Have to keep reminding myself I'm the boss not a boyfriend. Then, on a whim, I decide to ask her to be my partner at the Leap Year Ball. Strike while the iron is hot before one of her boyfriends does. She's very impulsive and says yes which is very satisfying considering the opposition. Then I hear from Dulcie that soon after she accepted my offer Wee Willie Jones from engineering asked her and so did Jim Ward, one of the scientists here who is also in the *Supersonics*. Just as well I was quick off the mark.

We are informed that the first production of the Sword for determining the depth of the submarine was also fitted into the *Hadleigh Castle* in the U.S. Since doing so we have had no trouble with it at all. On the strength of the trials the Americans have finally had to admit that our Sword Asdic set with its depth determining capability would be an advantageous piece of tackle to fit into their vessels. In fact, the trials went so well that they also begin to develop their own version.

Apparently it is freezing in New York but it is bad here too. The constant cold is certainly my mother's most common complaint and she says that as she cannot bear to stand in a queue for fish for two hours only to find there is none she has given up trying. So she is living instead on curried root vegetables as there is nothing fresh and green on offer. With a renewal of her worries about my health she sends me some woollen socks and a scarf she has knitted for my birthday and, when I do turn 28, I wear them with gratitude as I walk up to Fairlie Burn mess for a celebratory drink with the chaps. And I have to admit whenever the weather is at its very worst I am even reduced to wearing them in my bed.

The Leap Year Ball is held in the Naval Officers Mess at the Marine Hotel and it turns out to be a very good do. Muriel is a jolly good dancer and excellent company. Over supper she tells me that when she told the other girls who she was going with, they said to her 'Watch out, he's been out with nearly every girl in the Establishment'. I think she was warning me but I laughed and said that I had heard about her other beau too. 'Touche', she replied with a laugh. She is quite a girl.

We can be fooled for a night that life is fun and forget momentarily that there is a war on but only too soon it is back to business. At the end of March we hear the absolutely awful news that the RAF have suffered heavy losses at Nuremberg. We are all despondent and a few of the younger staff are worried their friends may have been shot down. Whilst we are so deeply involved in upgrading our gear we forget that German scientists are doing the same. Their Radar has obviously improved with devastating effect.

A Fairlie Burn lunch with the scientists and naval officers
Standing: Muriel, Vig, Eric (behind), Anderson and naval officers

Then, back at the Establishment after lunch one day, a bit of a shock. Roberts is dead. It is rumoured that it was an incurable condition but it has taken us by surprise because he is, was, only in his late forties. As none of us are in the front line we are not as used to the death of a colleague as those in the services and so we are all walking around wondering if it can be true. We know how much the loss must affect his family but, as so often happens during this war, we soon become pragmatic and realise that unfortunately it means one less pair of hands at the pumps and one less mind to come up with creative solutions to design problems.

30. Childhood Observations: South Africa, 1925

Vervet monkeys in the trees at Umgeni

There are any number of creative solutions to problem solving that I experienced during my childhood. And I now realise that this was something that came naturally to me and has since served me well in my experimental work. Perhaps it was because although the attention of my parents was focussed on me, an only child, I was nevertheless left to my own devices and I created my own interests.

Living in Durban, we often drove up to the Umgeni River to see the Vervet monkeys. Living in troops they would squeal to alert their companions if anyone came. The largest male was the boss and gave the orders. During the daytime they were extremely active, noisy and excited. Mom would say they reminded her of a group of small boys. And to tease her Dad would wink at me and say that as they never stopped talking and chattering they were more like a group of women.

This sort of remark never failed to madden Mom. I had always longed for one of these monkeys as a pet. The native people had an ingenious method of catching them. Cutting a very small hole in a pumpkin they scooped out most of the seeds. Then they left the hollowed out pumpkin on the ground and hid. Soon the small monkeys ventured out of the trees to look at it. One would climb all over it and peer into the hole, then sniff it and smell the tempting seeds.

Finally, the monkey would put its hand into the pumpkin to grab a fistful of seeds and at that very moment the men in hiding beat loudly on drums. Getting a shock the monkey froze and did not open its hand, keeping tight hold of the seeds. With its hand closed as a fist it could not pull it out of the pumpkin and with its fist stuck in the hole it could not run away. So, by observing the monkey's behaviour, the men were able to come up with a method to easily catch it. I have always remembered the process - close observation and a simple method is often the most effective way to solve a problem.

So that is where I got my monkey. A local man gave it to me although I suspect Dad paid for it. I kept her in the yard at home in our house in Cato Road. She was very attractive to look at with her white eyebrows and whiskers and a little black face. Her limbs were long, her tiny hands and feet were black and her fur was rough and a brownish grey but pale and whitish under the belly.

Joseph helped me to put a collar round her neck and a belt with a chain around her middle. The chain was attached to a pole with a loop and on top of the pole was a box shelter. It was how everyone kept their pet monkeys in those days. The pole was seven feet high and – I measured it – she could run all around the pole in a ten foot circle. I called her Puzzle after the Monkey Puzzle tree. Not very original but I was only eight or nine years old.

I generally fed Puzzle fruit but I also gave her seeds and leaves. Vervet monkeys also eat insects and spiders and pests like mice so she was quite useful in that way. But she ate eggs too and even young birds if she got into their nests and she was very partial to Mom's favourite Gardenia flowers. Along our road was a park and when Mom was out shopping or playing Bridge and Dad was at his office I would take Puzzle out for walks on a lead, which was great fun when old ladies realised it was not a nice little dog but a monkey that was coming up to them. And she was my willing partner in crime if I knocked an orange off a neighbour's tree of pinched a fig.

Puzzle was certainly very good company and made me laugh but I had to watch her because she was a terrible thief. She got to places one would never think possible because she was very agile and good at climbing and jumping. Mom made us move the pole further and further away from the house because things kept disappearing off the veranda. Pieces of fruit, boxes of matches, chocolates, pencils and hairpins all went missing. Small monkeys like Vervets will get their hand through any aperture and can manage to open boxes and drawers.

Unfortunately, when she was excited she chattered constantly and loudly and it eventually drove Mom mad. I was warned that if I did not control Puzzle she would have to go. I loved Puzzle and was desperate to keep her so I was forced to find a solution and soon devised a method of calming her. Over several days I had observed Puzzle's behaviour and noticed that when she was grooming herself she was at her most quiet. If her chattering became too noisy or went on for too long, I would call her to me by making a clicking noise. Then I sat on the floor beside her and separated her fur into partings. She allowed me to do this for anything up to half an hour at a time and she kept quite still while I did so. She obviously thought I was another monkey grooming her for fleas and she calmed down and kept very quiet.

From about the age of eight, when my parents were out I was allowed to do what I wanted. A favourite pastime of mine was to hide behind the poinsettia hedge that surrounded our garden and peer out - unobserved - at those passing by. I would watch the Indian fruit seller for the entire length of the road as he walked down selling his fruit. It fascinated me. He had baskets attached to each end of two bamboo slips tied together which he carried like a pair of scales over his shoulder.

The baskets of fruit would be very heavy when he started out. They bounced up and down as he walked. And after watching him over the months I was eventually able to explain to my parents how he managed to carry so much. He took each step forward when his baskets were at their height and therefore light in weight. Then they bounced down and he took the next step when they again bounced upwards. Eventually I asked him if this was so and he confirmed that it was. He said he had been taught it as a boy.

As time went on I was allowed to wander on my own. We could look down on the harbour from our road and I would walk down to the dry dock to see the vessels being worked on. Nobody was strictly allowed in there unless they were employed but – perhaps because I was small and did not pose a threat – I would slip in, chat to the men who were working on the boats and learn a great deal about them.

At weekends Dad would drive us to Riverside where we would often meet friends. Situated at the Umgeni river mouth it was a wonderful nature park where we could boat and fish. In the reeds and grasses all along the river banks one could see the most interesting birds. With Dad's racing binoculars and my bird book we would observe and identify them together. The larger birds – herons, storks and ospreys - could be seen at the water edge standing still as statues as we passed silently by in our boat.

At low tide Dad and I would wade out to the sandbanks and get closer to the small birds. The plovers would run away from us through the shallow water on their on their spindly legs and we could peer into their nests on the ground, lined with grass and with usually three speckled eggs they were perfectly camouflaged. Terns – in large groups – roosted on the sandbanks at low tide but flew up in masses if disturbed and we would watch them as they wheeled and wove through the air and dived for fish.

I think that my ability to observe closely and wait quietly to see what would happen was fostered during these days and certainly my love of wildlife and water was nurtured then. Both of my parents thought I was clever — in spite of my difficulties with reading and writing - and never worried about my mind, which was allowed to freely go and grow where it would.

Mrs. Alexander, Eric & Phil Alexander, 1926

Although never demonstrably loving, throughout my childhood my mother constantly, incessantly, worried about my health. My father, on the other hand, was demonstrative in his love for me and tried to temper my mother's worrying by boosting my confidence and doing everything he could to help me achieve my goals. He was a talented and competitive sportsman and an astute business man but these attributes were counterbalanced by his kindness and gentleness. I miss him still.

31. Sink or Swim:
Scotland, April - June 1944

Postcard of a U25 German U-boat

There are quite a few new girls here over the last few months and I must say it does make life much more enjoyable. There are eight of them, all very bright and capable. It has however been quite an eye opener for them to find out how security conscious we are and it takes them a little while to get used to being quizzed about where they are going and with whom. Even having a seemingly innocent and casual drink in an hotel or a bar can attract the attention of a naval security chap.

At first all the girls were accommodated in the YMCA in Largs because the Admiralty had no facilities for them. However, since then the Navy has taken over two hotels, Queens Hotel for the women, the Windsor for men, as billets. Although the girls are now in the hotel they say they were actually better off in the YMCA because for thirty bob a week they got accommodation and food. At the hotel the girls only get a billeting allowance and it doesn't go so far. They claim to be always hungry. Certainly - on the odd occasion I do eat lunch in the canteen - I am amazed at how much they can tuck away. Of course, it is cold up here and that does tend to give one an appetite.

All of our research here at the Establishment is at present 'High Priority'. Our Asdic gear is fully operational for D-Day now, the planned invasion of mainland Europe. Willis has been working on the HDA to locate underwater obstacles whilst I have developed an Asdic set for the 'X' Craft. I have also been working on a magnetostrictive transducer that will operate at 10Kc/s to facilitate underwater signalling between a parent submarine and small surface craft.

For many months now - apart from the Asdic set to guide the submersible forward - I have been refining a secondary Asdic set comprising an echo-sounder to determine the depth of the water below the keel in order to sense the ocean floor. This will allow the submersible to stay on the ocean floor until it is safe for it to surface. This is similar to the one used in Operation SOURCE when *Tirpitz* was damaged but with some adaptions.

In tandem I am also working on oscillators for other secondary Asdic sets. These are required for surface craft so they are able to detect underwater obstacles and the sea bed, in addition to an echo ranging set that can locate obstacles on the beach such as fencing. Throughout the last months the planned invasion of Europe is what most of us have been planning for and all that is discussed by everyone at meetings. I have also been developing a oscillator suitable for a marker buoy so am as busy as I have ever been.

However, there are still issues with these that need solutions. Muriel is still helping me for a couple of days a week. We test the oscillators together, first in air with her recording the results, then we put the oscillators in a tank of water and read off those pings. A cathode ray tube is wired up to an electrical source which has wires up to the tank to give impulses. I read the pings off the cathode ray tube and Muriel sits with a chart with x and y co-ordinates and as I read them she marks them on the chart. One evening last week, after she had returned from a Sunday trip home to Glasgow, I had read off several of these and thought it odd there was no response from her. I looked up and there she was, fast asleep sitting on a lab stool, pencil resting on her chart. A girl asleep looks so innocent and vulnerable but asleep whilst sitting on a lab stool, now that shows real skill.

Her other talent is singing and acting it seems. She and several of the girls are in the *Supersonics* production about to be staged. I am not really interested but of course I must be supportive and go and see the play when it's on in Largs. It's called, 'Middle Watch'- not new but I've not seen it before - set on a ship in peace time. Both the leading ladies are new to the cast, which must have raised an eyebrow or two. Mary McKechnie is one of the leads and Muriel the other. They play two flighty young women who get stranded on board a cruiser overnight. The Commander (Tom Emerson) and the Captain (Norman Astbury) then have to explain away their presence to the Admiral (Dennis Flann). The girls can sing alright. Altogether they were jolly good and it was fun to see Emerson and Astbury in uniform, acting.

But I think that Muriel's boyfriend, Jim Ward, who was playing the Flag Lieutenant was a bit wooden. Not very good at all. George was a very good General Manager, obviously, because it all went smoothly. His girlfriend, Rita Dawson, (who tells me that she only does it to see George), wasn't too bad and Don Herbert did an excellent job producing as usual. Must be his photographers' eye. It's being put on again in West Kilbride and I take Laura and Dulcie Boyle to see it, as a suitable way of repaying their hospitality.

I realise that I will have to actively woo Muriel away from the competition. Inviting her to dinner one Saturday at the Grosvenor in Glasgow, I introduce her to cocktails – she has an orange gin – which is fun and we go dancing afterwards at the Plaza where I have arranged for us to meet up with George and Rita, whose parents live at Pollock Shields. Muriel is a very good dancer which makes me appear to be better than I am. Afterwards she thoughtfully catches a tram alone back to Mosspark to stay the night with her parents so that the rest of us can go straight to Central Station to catch the last train back to Largs.

News from home and the wider world does register with us in spite of the Establishment being so introspective. The miners' strike is finally settled which must be a relief for the authorities. Not so much for us and our own comfort as sooner or later (probably the latter) the weather will warm up here but the effect on manufacturing — especially for armaments — must have been of real concern for the government. Stories of the ghettoes in Germany were bad enough but now even worse ones about concentration and extermination camps are filtering through. When will it end. We bury ourselves in our own work which helps to blot these fears out.

By mid-May we are overloaded with more High Priority work — we may have done all we can for the D-Day operation but we have still to come up with solutions to counteract deep diving U-boats. All this creative thinking and detailed research can fry my brain and so to keep my mind functioning I make sure I do get out on Sundays — and even have the occasional Saturday afternoon and odd evening off. Now that she has no more rehearsals, Muriel also has more free time so on those evenings we go to several local dances together. She whistles or constantly sings snatches of the new Noel Coward songs which has rekindled my love of that type of music.

As I am not so keen to share her with Americans in smart uniforms who can jitter-bug like movie stars, I prefer to take her to the cinema. I always put one of my chocolate bars in my pocket as Muriel has a very sweet tooth and I joke that she only comes with me for my stash. I must say, it is going down at an alarming rate though and I will have to come up with something when it does finally run out. She has told me that it is far superior to American chocolate bars but I don't ask how she knows.

This May is the warmest I have experienced here and it is a pleasure to be able to walk out across the moors. Some days, if I close my eyes and feel the sun on my face, I can almost believe I am back in the Cape.

By late May it is so hot that the girls have taken to swimming in their lunch break. Jo and I wander down too, for a bit of fresh air. We lean against the wall and watch the girls, in colourful bathing suits and swimming caps, dive off the pier. Jo points one out to me, 'That w'ane wi the thighs, I rather fancy her,' he says nudging me. 'Hey, hands off,' I say, 'I've got my eye on her!' I see that I shall have to up my game as Muriel is clearly a very popular girl. I immediately ask her if she would like to come with me to see a film at the Viking Cinema in Largs.

In preparation for D-Day we hear that the whole of the south coast has been earmarked a Defence Area. Captain Dendy, who has been down there, tells us that the whole area between Plymouth and Southampton and beyond is like one large military camp. It is awash with American troops and vehicles, British squadrons setting up camp and the strictest security measures in place. The Germans must know that it is on the cards.

We are aware that all leave for service men up here has been cancelled and so in the labs and offices we know that the operation is imminent. Then we know roughly when the day of the Operation is finally on us. Discreet calls to the design office, to us here in the labs, all followed by a complete security shut down. On 6th June we hear that Rome has fallen the previous day. We are winning in Italy, what a good sign we think.

Then the next day we hear that the D-Day landings started on the 6th. I have never known the Establishment so subdued. It is not the time to celebrate. There is hardly a person here who will not have some friend, family member or loved one involved and whom – in the worst case - may not survive the operation. For the next day or two we stay close to our desks and our benches, keep our thoughts to ourselves, go straight home in the evenings and listen to the wireless.

The landings began at dawn and the big surprise was that they did not take place at Calais, as everyone – including the Germans – were led to expect but on the Normandy beaches. Apparently there was a forward party to secure strategic bridges, but then hundreds of paratroopers landed behind enemy lines whilst coastal defences were bombed by our aircraft and blasted by our ships. British, Commonwealth, American and French troops then landed along a sixty mile stretch of coast.

During all of this at the Establishment we hope that our various Asdic detectors - on which we have worked so long - did their bit in helping the thousands of Allied troops get safely ashore. Whether it was our gear on Royal Naval ships, minesweepers, object detectors or in the midget 'X' Craft submarines guiding the vessels to shore, we hope that our Asdic sets did their job.

The news of the invasion – we are only now beginning to appreciate what an absolutely amazing and complicated piece of organisation and manpower that was - and battles proceed for a week. All of us are horrified and shaken when we see the pictures in the newspapers and hear reports of the casualties on the beaches during the landings. How many friends and family will be affected. How many lives changed forever. Allies, once again able to fly from French airfields, lull us into thinking that this indicates what will shortly be the end. Spirits palpably rise at the Establishment. We are hoping that this means it will all be over by the autumn.

Then, only a week after the Allied landings, German flying bombs land on England. The missiles look like miniature planes and are launched from sites along the French coast. Called V1's – easier to say than *Vergeltungswaffen* – they are falling on the London suburbs. My mother says she was shocked at first. By the time I realise the danger and telephone she says that they have been falling for a couple of days but that by now most people know how to react. If she can hear the engine then they are still going over but if that engine noise cuts out then it is necessary to run like greased lightening for shelter. I cannot see my mother ever running that fast but fear is probably quite an incentive. By the 20th they are falling night and day and my mother is annoyed that there are no alerts and even less information.

The missiles have already been nicknamed buzz bombs, or

doodlebugs, because of the noise they make. 'I thought all this was over with,' says my mother. 'We try and treat them as annoying insects and just get on with our daily tasks but they are actually destructive killers and I am already fed up to the back teeth with them.' Come up to Scotland, I say. 'Scotland is farther away than France!' 'By the time I get up there the Germans will have run out of supplies,' she replies. I take that as a no.

We are increasingly learning of the awful losses involved during the Normandy landings – fully aware of the unimaginable devastation inflicted on families – but count our blessings that our forces achieved their goal and that life for most of us might return to normal in the not too distant future. Meanwhile, in our research labs we continue as before trying to ameliorate the same old problems.

One problem we need to solve as a matter of urgency is that in the North Atlantic U-boats are diving increasingly much deeper than 900 feet to avoid Asdic attacks. We have modified oscillators to cope with this but now it is quite obvious that a complete redesign of Asdic (Top Secret) is necessary to come up with oscillators and a depth determining set that can deal with U-boats diving deeper to avoid detection. They simply sink to great depth and remain there, eluding our current equipment when under attack. Our research and development here has always been on a short term basis as we have needed to come up with solutions quickly during the most hectic and serious period of U-boat threats.

To date we have managed to modify equipment to deal with U-boats diving to a maximum of 900 feet but deeper than that – 1,200 feet is suggested although they may already be capable of diving in excess of 1,500 feet - will mean a complete redesign. A new set will be a step change for us as it will inevitably be long term, taking many, many months of work and for which we will need submarines to simulate U-boats that are capable of these speeds and depths in order to carry out trials. I can see I will be up there in Tobermoray for many months to come.

The other big worry is that many U-boats, as a further method of avoiding detection, are now fitted with *Schnorkel*, a tube that allows the submarine, whilst just below the surface, to expel carbon (diesel exhaust) and draw in oxygen. This allows the U-boat - whilst submerged at perhaps only 150 feet - to travel at speed and, very importantly, submerged in this way the U-boats evade Radar. Now we have, in effect, both fast and deep submarine to counteract.

Muriel tells me that she is going on holiday to Rothesay with her family at the beginning of July. Apparently her father refuses to go away during the last two weeks of July because that is when the Glasgow factory workers have their holiday and he wants to avoid it. She says she will only go for one week and I say I hope she will have a good time. And, for the first time ever, I do wonder whom I will confide in, whom I will tease and talk to when she is not here. Before she leaves we walk up the hillside to Fairlie Burn, paddling barefoot in the cool peaty stream until we reach Fairlie Glen. Drying our feet on the heather we climb further until we reach Fairlie Moor. As we sit together having a kiss and a cuddle I admit that I will miss her, very much, and Muriel asks if I would like to visit her when she is on holiday. Because, she says, she will miss me dreadfully too. It is suddenly clear that we feel just as strongly about each other. When I see her off on her bus to make the journey back to Glasgow the fact that we will see each other in a few days makes the parting less melancholy.

'Middle Watch' the *Supersonics* production with Muriel centre stage

The next week Jock Anderson calls me into the office to say that he wishes to inform me that I am promoted. Could this be because not one ship was lost during the D-Day landings due to the success of not only heavy air coverage but also our excellent Asdic screen. Or could it be the Asdic fitted in the 'X' Craft that helped get men and craft ashore, I wonder. I only say it is news that I was being considered but welcome news. I am actually thrilled and am now a (Temporary) Senior Experimental Officer. At 28 years old the youngest yet according to Vig.

My title is, 'Head of Research Group on piezoelectric and magnetostrictive transducers and on the mechanical and acoustic properties of sonar domes'. I will also have over twenty extra staff under me as will now be officially responsible for the oscillator design and production team as well as my scientific assistants. Plus a rise in salary, which is welcome. I wish Muriel was here to share such satisfactory news.

32.   All Change:
Scotland, July – September 1944

Postcard of Rothesay Bay and the Cowal Hills

I catch the bus up to Largs and get the first ferry on Saturday morning. The trip over to the Isle of Bute stirs memories of the ferry over to St Lucia although the scale is totally different. There is the same sense of hands on, hope we get across, ramshackle sort of feel to it. Possibly because the ferry is very old and not too fast. All the better paddle steamers and ferries have been requisitioned for war work. Keeping carefully to our lanes to avoid mines we make for Toward Point, the impressive Cowal Hills in the distance, but turn beforehand into the Kyles of Bute, which separate the Isle from the Argyll mainland.

This is the beautiful landscape of soft coloured slopes and silvery lochs that Scots all over the world hang on their walls. All that is needed is for a large stag with a full set of antlers to appear on the horizon. I have been up here many times to do trials in Loch Striven - and even

Port Bannatyne where the midget subs are based - but it is the first time I will land at Rothesay, the only town on the island.

HMS *Cyclops*, the depot ship for the submarine flotilla, is moored in the bay - a hive of activity with tugs and small craft buzzing around it, sailors climbing onboard from one of the submarines alongside, a few off duty Wrens hanging over the bows watching a diver doing some maintenance on the water line - but my eyes are drawn beyond it to the terminal and old wooden pier where Muriel is waiting. I feel a lift when I see her, a quickening of the pulses, excitement. Basically pleasure, I suppose. Then desire when I put my arm around her, kiss her. She is just a little reserved, a bit Scottish, which makes me fancy her even more. Funny the Scots. At the drop of a hat they will tell any stranger their every personal detail but balk at displaying any outward show of affection in public to even the closest family member.

Muriel says that her younger brother and little sister wanted to come down to meet me but she promised instead to bring me up for lunch. Inevitably that means meeting her mother and father too. Several of the hotels have been requisitioned by the Royal Navy and she says there is plenty in the way of entertainments in town – cinemas, music at the Winter Gardens or dancing at places like the impressive new Pavilion on the seafront – for holiday makers and service personnel alike. And for us if I want that. But I say I would prefer it if we could spend time alone together and, when she gives me a wide smile and squeezes my hand, I know this is what she wants too.

So we ignore the holiday crowds and the troops everywhere (of every nationality it seems) and make our way out of town. We clamber up the rugged hillside, sometimes my pushing her, her pulling me, and pick our way along the sheep trails until we reach the castle. Sitting up there on a boulder, the wind brushing by, the clouds floating over and one feels a sense of release. I suppose we take the stress and feeling of urgency so much for granted that we only notice when away from it all.

At the small cottage where Muriel's family are staying I meet her parents. Her father, an ex-army major, upright and moustached (although a little portly) and her mother, statuesque and as tall as her husband, greet me very formally. But the children - her brother mischievous, her sister curious – are fascinated by this stranger. Muriel's mother cooks us brown trout, caught this morning in Loch Fad, that fried in precious butter are delicious. I feel that I am on parade – here to be vetted.

Afterwards, we offer to take the children with us as a way of escape and go down to the Children's Corner on the coast where we sit and talk, watching some holiday makers attempting to fish from small skiffs in the bay - or trying to conquer their oars and make for the shore - while the children paddle and play in the sand. After an hour or so Mr. Mckinnon comes to collect them and we have at last some time alone together before I have to take the ferry back to Largs.

On the day Muriel is due to return we hear the news that the Russians have crossed into Poland. We none of us can imagine what that will mean but hope that the Soviet troops will be less bloody than the Germans. When Muriel comes up to see me in the lab she tells me that after I returned to the mainland her mother said, 'Well, he's not very bonny, but he has got something,' which she seems to find very funny. Considering the Scots and their ability for understatement and inability to praise, it is probably as close to a compliment as one can hope for. I think I must have passed inspection.

At one time there were virtually no young women in Largs, now there are hundreds of them. The Moorings opposite Largs pier - a nautical looking hotel complete with railings and flagpole - has been requisitioned as the shore base, HMS COPRA. For those not in the know that is Combined Operations Pay, Ratings and Accounts for the Royal Navy pay office. Hundreds of Wrens and Petty Officers have been moved up here from London and work in teams doing the salary admin and calculating the pay due to service men.

The Wrens are all billeted in the Skelmorie Hydro Hotel and in huts in its grounds a few miles north of the town so there is a steady fleet of buses delivering Wrens morning, noon and night to Largs, Skelmorie and every point north, south and east. The single chaps here perked up no end when they realised that there were so many young women around but the Wrens only get Sunday afternoons off. Consequently, although there must be a couple of hundred available girls, it is either too far for the single chaps to go or there is too little time to woo them.

We are working – still – on rubber samples because now (there is always some new threat) the Admiralty is more worried than ever that the Germans have got one over on us. For some time now a number of U-boats have been covered in rubber tiles to avoid Asdic detection although these have never been wholly successful as they have a tendency to fall off. This may be due to the tile material becoming brittle or due to inferior adhesion. We have been aware of this for some time but the Germans have been experimenting with rubber sheeting to encase the outside of their hulls for a while now and this appears to be more efficient.

The sheeting like the tiles will not only deflect Asdic beams but will have the secondary benefit of deadening the sound of the engines. I have therefore been developing the use of Neoprene, a synthetic polymer that has a different chemical structure. It is resilient at very low temperatures and can be produced as large flat sheets that do not fracture when bent. This is essential if it is to be used to encase our own vessels.

More urgently, however, the most pressing worry for the Admiralty is the lack of good quality quartz without which we will not be able to produce or develop our Asdic sets further. This is a problem and I have mentioned it in my reports to the Admiralty. Not long after I joined the Establishment I started work on magnetostrictive transducers as an alternative to piezoelectric quartz oscillators because they can be effective in some cases and are easier to produce. However, when highly sensitive measurements are required with a high level of accuracy and less audible noise (as in the Asdic sets that track U-boats) then a higher frequency is needed which only the piezoelectric quartz oscillators can reliably supply.

Worryingly, there is a shortage of good quality quartz with which to produce them so an alternative quartz-like material is required that has piezoelectric qualities. Ammonium dihydrogen phosphate (ADP) crystals could be the answer. In the U.S. they have already replaced their alternative for quartz (Rochelle Salt) with ADP crystals for use in their transducers. My noise measurement tests on samples from the States have shown that they have a wide frequency response. ADP crystals would not only be a great deal cheaper to use and easier to handle than quartz but could also be readily available if we grew our own supplies.

Eric Pratt, having been in the U.S. and visited labs such as NRL and Bell Telephones, is fully aware of the importance of this material and is hoping to convince the Admiralty that it is essential that we learn how to grow the crystals ourselves. We have done various experiments on man-made crystals along these lines but the Americans have the technology already developed and it would be nonsensical if we did not ask them to show us their production methods. Speed is, after all, of the essence.

Pratt says that if he gets the go ahead would I, as Head of Oscillator Research, be willing to go over to the U.S. and learn their technique. I jump at the idea because it would be fascinating to see their crystal growing techniques and a wonderful chance to look at any other research or methods of production they have. We shall have to wait and see and meantime I carry on as usual.

Then some very good news indeed, Paris is liberated! By all accounts, as the Allies approached Paris, the French workers went on strike, built barricades and shot at German soldiers. The Allies managed to dissuade the Germans from burning the city down and a few days later General Eisenhower (diplomatically allowing the French army to enter the city first) liberated Paris. On the wireless we hear that British, American, Canadian and French troops all celebrate this victory in grand style.

This is followed by our own little success. The Admiralty are pleased to inform us that our old friend, HMS *Loch Killin,* has sunk the first U-boat using Squid. Such excellent news and so satisfying to get a result from all our hard work. If the war comes to an end soon our success with Squid will be too late to make the sort of difference we could have done with back in 1942, '43 but, on the other hand, we are ready for whatever may come our way next.

Lulled into a false sense of security by all this we are taken unawares when Jerry decides to give us another dose of his medicine. To show us what he can do before he is finally pushed out of France he sends over a rocket more dreadful and destructive than the flying bomb. The first V2 lands in England on the 8th September and immediately causes real fear. My mother is on the telephone every day. For the first time she is thoroughly shaken. 'This is the last straw!' she says with feeling. 'These new doodlebugs make no noise, there's no warning, they just suddenly go bang. Silent killers.' She has finally had enough and agrees that the quiet west coast of Scotland may be more comfortable than noisy, bombed out London. Although I offered, I am nevertheless not quite prepared for such a rapid about turn and have to find accommodation double quick.

Muriel's mother has a friend, Molly Grant, who has a two bedroom flat - number 2 Hutton Park - in Largs that she would be only too happy to rent out. I jump at the chance, give Mrs. Hutton notice, and take the flat for my mother and myself. The bonus is that I will travel to work every day with Muriel. When I go to the station to meet my mother I wonder if the flat will be big enough as she is accompanied by two large trunks, four suitcases and several bags.

On the very same day we hear that RAF Lancaster bombers have attacked the *Tirpitz* and scored a hit but, unfortunately, not sunk her. Will that blasted battlecruiser never die, I ask myself. And on the following day I hear from Pratt. He and I are to go to the States as soon as we can arrange visas and we may be away for a few months. It is all happening at break neck speed. I tell my mother about Muriel — which gets a mixed reception - and ask her for the sapphire and diamond ring she promised me (aged 12) was destined for my wife.

I explain that I cannot possibly risk waiting until I get back because on my return I may find such a popular girl as Muriel engaged to someone else – Peter Ward who works with me sometimes has already made a pass at her. Quite apart from the fact that I am about to run out of chocolate bars. My mother comes up with every reason why I should not get married but I remind her that due to my recent promotion I am in a strong financial position and that Muriel will keep her company in the flat whilst I am away in America. Deciding, possibly, that she will have financial security and a home with us, she hands over the ring.

On the 24th September I put the ring and my last chocolate bar in my pocket and take Muriel out for a fancy dinner. I tell her that in less than a month I go to America for a few months - her clear blue eyes fill with tears and I know I must not lose her – but that I'd like us to be married before we go. She looks at me with a beautiful smile that lights up her face. I tell her that I love her, that I want to share my life and all my worldly goods with her. I empty my pockets and ask her which she wants, the small box in my right hand or the chocolate bar in my left. But I have met my match. She says that as I am about to promise her all my worldly goods she would like both.

Muriel, Fairlie Glen 1944

33. A Crystal Radio Receiving Set: London, 1923

Postcard of SS *Ceramic*

The doctor told Mom that there was no one in South Africa that could help me when my throat was very bad. He thought I had something called tubercular glands and said that the only person who could help was a specialist in this type of illness and the specialist was in London. Dad and Mom decided that it was essential that I was seen by this man and that Dad would stay at work in Durban and Mom and I would go to England. So at seven years old I travelled to England for the first time. Mom and I sailed on the SS *Ceramic*, of the White Star Line, via Madeira to Southampton and from there to the Regent Park Hotel in London.

At our stop in Madeira Mom made the most of the shopping opportunity and bought several hand embroidered tablecloths and linen table mats. I was bribed to be patient with the promise of an ice-cream and a ride on one of the horse drawn sleds. But crossing the equator was the most exciting thing that happened on the journey for me. The crew made the celebrations the greatest fun and left me with the strongest feeling that the best way to travel was by ship.

When we saw the Consultant in London he said I had to be admitted in the German Hospital. It was part of St Bartholomew's Hospital but was situated in Hackney. Off we went and I was left there in charge of a rather fierce lady. It was a very large ward and I was inspected by doctors who said I had to have hot flannel strips wrapped around my neck. They were changed every day and the only thing I was allowed to eat was porridge. Unfortunately, it had lumps in it the size of walnuts and inside the lumps the oats were dry which made them very difficult to swallow. Awful.

I don't know how long I was in that hospital but it felt like a very long time. Every afternoon Mom caught a bus to come and see me but she was not allowed to stay for very long. The rest of the time I could only lie in bed although sometimes I was allowed to get out of the bed and sit in a chair and look at books and weeklies. I really missed Dad and being at home. I thought that England was a very grey place: the December sky was grey, the roads were grey, the buildings were grey and the blanket on my bed was scratchy and grey.

When I was in hospital Mom visited one of Dad's twin sisters, Henrietta, who had recently given birth to a son. Mom said that Hetty was very welcoming and that I could meet the family when I was better and everyone was sure that I had nothing infectious. Dad knew her husband because they had both been members of the same boxing club in London. Apparently it was the same boxing club that Barnay Barnato, the South African mining millionaire, had trained in when he lived in London. I think Dad was hoping that the same good fortune would happen to him.

I was very glad when finally they did say that I could go home and Mom was very relieved. My glands were not tubercular after all. At last I could see London and meet Dad's British relatives. I had no brothers and sisters so the thought of English cousins was quite exciting. Aunt

Hetty's husband, Hymie Freedman, now trained boxers and was a physiotherapist. When he saw me he said that I was undernourished and wasting away. He offered to massage my muscles back to health. Mom said that he certainly seemed to have healing hands as I rapidly regained strength and was soon running around like any normal boy of my age.

Hetty's mother, my grandmother, lived in Whitechapel and we caught a bus there from our hotel on Piccadilly. The first thing my grandmother Rosenthal did when she met me was to give me a present. It was a brown leather purse with a small E on it. Mom said the delicate initial was gold and that I should take great care of it. But I remember I was more pleased with the silver three penny bit inside it. Dad's eldest sister, Lizzie, was a widow and Dad was keen that Mom and I met up with her and her three children when we came to England. He said she needed all the help and support we could give since her husband had died two years earlier. He had been an electrician and at the age of 39 had been electrocuted when up a ladder. Henry was her eldest child, Esther was a year older than me and Seymour was only three.

It was arranged for us all to meet at my grandmother's house when the whole family would be there to admire Henry's tenth birthday present. And it was then that I learnt something quite marvellous. Henry had been given a crystal radio receiving set. It was made by Meccano and came in a carton for him to build himself. There were a few things that were not included so Aunt Hetty bought him the cat's whisker and the crystal. Her twin, Aunt Rhoda, bought him the flat fibre base plate and the telephone receiver to go with the set.

Henry showed me how he had already joined two perforated Meccano plates together with small nuts and bolts which he had attached to the flat fibre base. Following the instructions he had then screwed small brackets to the perforated tin plates and these in turn had been screwed into all the pieces according to the drawings. He carried on following the instructions for the wiring whilst I watched and then he carefully mounted the important crystal in two double brackets. Lastly, he wired the single telephone receiver to the set.

Finally, when Henry finished making his crystal radio receiving set, he was ready to try it out. The whole family sat around the room and watched. It was then that something happened that I would never forget. Henry turned the set on and when the tip of the wire (called the cat's whisker) touched the surface of the little crystal rock contact was made and the signal was picked up. That was when I heard the words, 'This Is London'. The words were transmitted by the British Broadcasting Company miles away. It was like magic. 'This Is London'. It was the first time I heard a radio.

At that time broadcasting stations across the country transmitted news bulletins and weather reports as well as music and stories. As Henry now had a receiving set – quite splendidly made entirely out of Meccano apart from a few small fittings – and as he lived within 25 miles of a broadcasting station, he was able to listen to these programmes in his own sitting room. Lots of boys all over England must have heard them and all due to little pieces of crystal rock that grew in countries from across the world.

Eric, aged 7

Once scientists had discovered that natural crystals could be used to detect radio signals without the use of electrical power people all over the country had begun to make their own homemade crystal sets in order to communicate. But none of us there that day had any experience of such things and so it was greatly exciting. Uncle Hymie put it into words, 'It is a wonderful science that allows radio transmission and reception'. My cousin, who was very precise, looked in the Meccano Magazine and told him it was actually called, 'Wireless Telephony and Telegraphy'.

34. Wedding Bells:
Scotland, October 1944

George Hodsman, Eric, Muriel and Betty Gillespie,
Glasgow, 6th October 1944.

Muriel and I catch the train to Glasgow Central Station to meet her parents, show them the ring and tell them that we have become engaged. A dram of whisky with Mr. McKinnon seals it and I go back to Fairlie whilst Muriel stays for the weekend. We want to get married straight away as experience has taught everyone we know not to delay important decisions. We have never discussed it, but my journey to America would not be without danger and if I am to become a cropper I want to enjoy married life no matter how brief.

Muriel told her parents that I am due to go to America within weeks and may be away for two months or so. Her father said, 'Oh, so you'll wait till he gets back' but Muriel replied, 'No, we'll get married next week before he goes.' Her father was apparently quite shocked but her mother is a very practical woman and said, 'You'd better get things organized then.'

We will not have time to get a special licence to get married in a registry office as that would need a three week notice period. However, the Session Clerk told Muriel that if the banns were read in the morning for the first time, then in the evening for the second and final time we can get married in the kirk the following week. Both Muriel and I are now registered as living at her parent's house and the service is arranged.

Mrs. McKinnon reasoned that the hotels would already be booked on a Saturday so advised that we married on a Friday. The Marlborough Hotel was immediately booked as they will let us have the maximum allowed number of guests – forty – and provide a meal. The only meal allowed in wartime costs a maximum of 10/6 per person so that is what we are having. However, no liquor can be bought in hotels (another wartime restriction) and as a result Mr. McKinnon has told Muriel that he has called in several favours to use their coupons to buy the whisky. He plans to bring it to the wedding breakfast at the hotel under wraps in a suitcase, which he says is now the preferred method of delivery. I will wear my 'interview' suit and Muriel is planning to buy herself a suit with her father's coupons and some new shoes with her grandfather's. Meanwhile, I buy an 18 carat gold wedding ring before learning that she would actually like one the same width as her engagement ring. I leave it with the jeweller to resize.

The war looms large as ever with sad news about the uprising in Poland. The Russians have ceased their half-hearted attempts to come to the aid of Warsaw and the Germans, able defeat the Polish resistance, have razed the city to the ground. Our RAF did their best to support the underground resistance but it needed whole-hearted support from the Russians too. Here in Britain we all feel relief – although we never put it into words - that although we have been bombed and so many of us killed we have not suffered the humiliation and cruelty associated with occupation. Nor have we starved.

The evening before the wedding I get wind of plans that the chaps at the Establishment have some thing or other in mind for me as I leave work. I can imagine all sorts of uncomfortable jinks happening to me – the sorts of thing I myself have carried out on other unsuspecting grooms – and I take avoiding action. Sliding open the window in my office, I climb out and make my way gingerly over the corrugated tin roof, down a drainpipe, across the yard and escape before anyone notices I have gone. When my mother and I get to Glasgow we catch a taxi to Muriel's Aunt Cathy with whom we are staying the night.

The ring I had bought for Muriel is still to arrive. Worried that it would not be ready in time for the ceremony, Cathy took the precaution of buying a faceted 9 carat gold one as a spare just in case. My ring is delivered as soon as we arrive in the morning but annoyingly - judging by Cathy's ring - it is also too small and not quite narrow enough. I spend the early hours of the following morning stretching it on the handle of a screwdriver and using emery paper to file it down in width and smooth it. I think that there are enough gold filings on the carpet to make another.

As soon as we were engaged I had asked George to be my best man and Muriel asked her cousin, Betty Gillespie, to be her maid of honour. As many of Muriel's friends are away on duty in the forces, our guests - apart from my mother and Muriel's family and friends – are friends from the Establishment: George's girlfriend, Rita Dawson, Hector and Marie Willis, Joe and Ethel Fisher, Jon and Margaret Johnson, Dennis and Cynthia Flann, Muriel's old room-mate at Queen's Hotel, Jean Bell, and Moshe Feldenkrais make up our party. Sadly, Vig is away.

Although Don Herbert, the Establishment's photographer, has been asked to take the official photographs, Moshe is insisting on taking some too as he says that in his opinion wedding photographs never seemed to catch the more intimate moments. So he takes a photograph of me putting the ring on Muriel's finger but thankfully he did not catch the earlier, very intimate, moment when I realise that the ring is still a tad too small and have to quickly lick the inside of it before pushing it onto

Muriel's finger. That evening we catch the train to travel up to the highlands. I find an empty carriage and pulling down the blinds onto the train corridor I loop my carnation buttonhole through the door handle and close the door. It works a treat and we are marvellously undisturbed until, finally, soon after Sterling, a lady knocks on the door and says plaintively, 'I'm so sorry but there is not another seat to be had on the train.'

Arriving at Fishers Hotel in Pitlochry I am very disappointed to find the room is not up to expectations and complain to the hotelier – much to Muriel's surprise and embarrassment – that we are not used to single beds. He apologises and finds us much better room with a double bed. At Aviemore, our next stop in the Cairngorms, I ask at the reception desk what sort of room it is before I take possession of the keys and by the time we reached Grantown-on-Spey I boldly say that I expect their best double room.

Our short honeymoon is over all too soon but we have enjoyed ourselves, and each other's company, and had bracing walks through the spectacular Cairngorms, into castles, up hills, down dales and over raging salmon rivers. Back from our trip the arrangements for my mission to the States are still in limbo. I have had to apply for a permit to visit the States – and had a photograph taken for it - but the Americans are being incredibly slow. Too much official red tape our chaps say - one would think there was no war on.

In the meantime Muriel and I resume our work; myself developing a retractable dome that is more streamlined to take into account fast U-boats in conjunction with working up my idea of a bottom contact set that could detect submarines by virtue of a shadowgraph effect whilst Muriel assists not only myself but Vig and the Wills' too. There is still the feeling that we have much to achieve although our research is not quite so all consuming and pressurised. When we get back to our flat at night my mother has produced some ingenious meal and I appreciate again what a good cook she is. On Sundays she shows Muriel how to make South African dishes and one weekend Muriel – to keep her own end up - makes Scottish scones and pancakes learnt from her own mother.

At the end of the month there is more news of *Tirpitz*. Moored outside Tromso in Norway since its last hit and, no longer seaworthy, it is being used as a floating gun battery. As such it can still inflict damage on our aircraft and ships. The RAF have not given up and have it in their sights and again the Lancaster's attack. Apparently with the bad weather once more and the anti-aircraft guns bombarding them meant that they did not get a hit. However, it seems that there was some damage when their Tallboy bombs exploded underwater close to the ship and that has rendered the vessel even less seaworthy than before. That blasted battlecruiser refuses to die.

35. The *Aquitania* : America, November 1944

Postcard of RMS *Aquitania*

At last my permit comes through and I am bound for America. Eric Pratt and I take the train from Largs to Glasgow and Greenock near to where we are to embark. I am not to mention that I am a scientist and am registered as a foreign official which is of course true. We are to travel on one of the great ocean liners that have been pressed into action – presently on continuous service - to transport troops across the oceans to and from the U.S.A.

The Cunard White Star Liner, RMS *Aquitania,* its four funnels and body now painted battleship grey, is at anchor off Gourock in the Clyde Estuary as the docks at Greenock are in use by the Royal Navy. It is also doubtful that they would be wide and deep enough for such a large liner anyway. Once it is dark we are warned to be as quiet as possible and are ferried out to the ship and – the crew and troops already on board – by 10pm weigh anchor and are underway, shortly passing through the boom at Gourock.

If we were hoping for a luxurious journey we are soon disenchanted. In peace time the boat is advertised as carrying 3,300 passengers in luxury with the most spacious and grand public reception areas. However, in converting it to war time use any space at all is a luxury. We immediately learn that it is carrying so many troops that all communal areas have been converted to other more practical uses and there is nothing luxurious whatsoever remaining.

The service men we are to share our berth with tell us that they expect us to be escorted and protected by surface vessels – most likely a convoy of cruisers - as we cross the Atlantic. Pratt and I say nothing as we are well aware that troopships like the *Aquitania* can travel fast (at 20 knots much faster than a destroyer and still able to out run a U-boat) and that it will probably be thought unnecessary to have an escort right the way across the vast expanse of the Atlantic ocean or to travel in convoy. So when the ships escorting us through British coastal waters and inner Western Approaches leave us neither he nor I are surprised that the ship continues alone. Zig zagging our way and changing direction constantly to avoid detection means it will take us much longer to cross but I value getting there in one piece.

The ship is positively brimming over with men. I remarked that it was packed and one of the U.S. servicemen said 'not nearly as bad as coming back from Australia when there were 22,000 of us men on board and there were three shifts with only 8 hours each in a bunk'. On board now there are women troops too – U.S. Women's Army Corps for example – but male and female troops are very tightly segregated on board. Having left Sydney and come via Cape Town the G.I's must be getting stir crazy so this is probably a very sensible precaution. With so many on board no-one can have a personal berth or even eat at the same time. Officers and big wigs - and women passengers - get slightly better berths above the water line but regular troops have tiers of four bunks in a cabin designed for one (or sleep in folding bunks in fairways) and have to share their bunk by sleeping in 12 hour rotas.

We find out on embarking that this will include Pratt and myself and that we too can only use our bunk for 12 hours a day and will have to eat in the same shifts as the troops. We join the long 'chow' lines and get two meals a day, 12 hours apart. Waiting to be served takes an age but at least we are above the water line and get respite from feeling incarcerated and the food is surprisingly good and portions generous. Tokens were issued to us when we embarked and these have to be produced at every mealtime. Like the service men on board we fill up between meals with chocolate bars – a treat for us – and savoury items from the snack shop.

Security is as tight as can be possible on such a crowded troopship. No cameras are allowed on board for obvious reasons and radios are banned in case their signal is picked up by the enemy. Rubbish is dropped overboard at sunset so that by daylight it cannot give our position away. At night the boat is strictly blacked out because quite obviously we do not want to be spotted by enemy craft of any description. The ship is armed against surface attack with guns facing forward and aft but these will be dismally inadequate should a German battlecruiser appear. The armaments I see against air attack look a little better with Bofors guns, cannons and rockets but they too will not be very successful against any number of enemy bombers. Instead the ship will mainly be relying on speed.

Regularly changing its course will help as will Radar and Asdic operators on top of their job. At night the Radar should detect any surfaced U-boats whilst there are plenty of keen eyed lookouts on duty by day. I am reminded of my deck vigils during the journey to Australia but this time it is not icebergs that I fear but torpedoes. Just one hit would slow us down to such an extent that further attacks would be sure to finish us off. I put my faith in the Asdic operators as they should be on constant alert for U-boats.

At least once so far the ship has shuddered as a result of firing an armament and suddenly turned away to take evasive action. It may have been real or it may have been a false alarm but I am reassured that everything is functioning on the Bridge. Everyone on the ship has in the back of their mind – and sometimes the forefront - that disaster can strike at any time. Because of this - and the fact that there are clearly insufficient life rafts to cope with so many passengers - we have to wear or carry our life jackets 24 hours a day which is far from comfortable or convenient. And for an hour every morning we all go on deck in relays for lifeboat drills which we all grumble at. However, the experience of a full blown gale a few days out convinces us of the need.

Washing facilities are also very limited on board and with so many men cramped into such a small place - and so many of them smokers - the air below is far from healthy. Free deck space is limited too but I make as much use of it as I can, walking up and down to the maximum extent always in the same direction as everyone else which is required to avoid tripping or causing a jam. To keep everyone occupied there are films and concerts around the clock interspersed with church services and, off course, our regular emergency drills.

As we live in such close proximity to the U.S. servicemen we are glad to swop news and chat to other civilians - on their way to the States for business not pleasure - we bump into. Otherwise Pratt and I play chess – I have brought a small travelling chess set - while the troops find a seat wherever they can, hunched on the floor in doorways or crouching in corners, playing board or card games. Gambling on any game is forbidden as it can incite arguments culminating in fights amongst the servicemen but I have seen dice games where the most ingenious betting does take place. And there is a strictly no alcohol policy for the same reason. There are nevertheless fights amongst the GI's every day so after six days of all this I am quite ready to disembark and so spend as much time as possible up on deck.

Thankfully, on the 9th November, we reach New York. What excitement on board when first an aircraft patrol flies overhead as the New York skyline comes into sight, then tugs come alongside as the vast

Statue of Liberty looms large over us dominating the harbour entrance. When finally a foghorn sounds our arrival, hundreds of men whoop and cheer, sing and wave. Jostled close to the railings on the deck next to a group of GI's, one of them tears off his life vest, "This is my last trip" he shouts above the din. He throws it with force across the railings into the sea, there are cheers and then, incredulously, we all watch it sink out of sight. As we glide up the Hudson in what must surely be one of the largest and longest ships in the world we are dwarfed by the Manhattan skyscrapers towering above us. The skyline is a fantastic sight, the tall Empire State Building recognisable amongst the many city buildings. It is awe inspiring.

At Brooklyn NY Pier 86, once the customs men have done their stuff, we finally disembark. I am not surprised that it is as freezing in New York as it is in Scotland – thank goodness I have my wool overcoat - and we go straight away to an hotel. Our expenses are fairly generous and so we can afford to stay in a reasonable one but although the hotel we find is not top notch it is positively luxurious after our time on board the boat. Whilst Pratt rests (sleep on the ship was fitful at best), I intend to see as much of the city as I can as I may not return through New York and tomorrow I shall have to fulfil the commissions to purchase various items for my mother and Muriel.

I walk through Madison Square Garden, see the Rockefeller Centre, Grand Central Station and visit the Empire State Building. Tired but determined - as there will be no time to take in a show - I walk down Broadway for a little way to get the feel of it so I can tell Muriel when I get home. Wandering the streets I am struck by the absence of bomb damage and sandbags but am awed by the height of the buildings, the enormous blocks and wide avenues. Fascinating too are the many races – Caribbean, Chinese, Russian, Italian - and the wide choice of food in the restaurants and bars. The colours, smells and accents so different from the wartime London I have got to know.

Lured by aromas I buy an eastern European snack from a street vendor and my taste buds re-awakened I look forward to sitting down in a restaurant for a full slap up meal. For this first evening both Pratt and I plump for an all American beef steak, potato fries and salad in a swish and brightly lit eatery nearby. The enormous steak is enough for two people – what a treat - and how wonderful and succulent it tastes. Afterwards we manage to get into a small jazz bar, dark and lively, where we are not permitted to buy our own drinks as everyone is fascinated by our accents and we are pumped for information about life in England.

The next morning I walk through Central Park and go to Macy's on Fifth Avenue - its Christmas decorations already strung up – the large department store my mother has stipulated where the glamour and variety of everything on offer amazes me. Following my instructions to the letter, I buy myself a grey suit (the material feels very thin to me) so that Muriel can use the 26 coupons it would cost me at home - a six month supply - instead. My mother has given specific details of the boned Gossard girdle she requires and I am very surprised (and amused) when a pretty shop assistant – much slimmer than my mother - models it for me in stockings and high heels. I also purchase 20 pairs of Rayon stockings and some Rayon pyjamas for Muriel. And Spence Mackay has asked if I can buy a teddy bear whilst I am here for his young son, Michael, which I do with pleasure.

Eric, visa photograph for the U.S.A., 1944

36. California and Crystals:
November – December 1944

Tirpitz is finally dead! I transcribe what I read in a newspaper after only a few days in America: "London November 13 – The 41,000 ton German Battleship *Tirpitz* last 'unsinkable' giant in Adolf Hitler's fugitive navy capsized and sank yesterday morning in the icy Norway waters of Tromso Fjord when hit squarely by three six ton 'earth-quake' bombs dropped by RAF Lancasters, the British announced tonight." What satisfying and wonderful news. At last.

It seems that on 12th November RAF Bomber Command sent 30 Lancaster bombers over to Norway where they finally finished *Tirpitz* off. I think of all the months of work perfecting our gear and the frustration that the operation was ineffective in that there was only slight damage inflicted. Our pilots must have felt the same after their previous abortive attempts to sink the brute but this highly successful mission must have erased those previous frustrations. It is such truly excellent news. Well done RAF. Pratt insists on accompanying me to San Diego although I understood that he would be going straight to the Research Stations in Canada. We take a plane to Salt Lake City and then onwards to San Diego. It is here that I shall find out the method they use in the U.S.A. to grow ammonium dihydrogen phosphate (ADP) crystals. An ADP crystal ($NH_4H_2PO_4$) is a single, transparent, piezoelectric crystal containing no water of crystallization. It occurs when a solution is added to ammonia and when enough has been added the liquid becomes distinctly acidic and it crystallizes in tetragonal prisms.

Oscillators using manmade single ADP crystals are much cheaper to fabricate than ones using natural quartz crystals and can be used in Asdic sets - or sonar transducers as the Americans prefer to refer to them. Quartz crystals are still preferable to use in some underwater sound projectors but the supply of Brazilian crystals large enough to be of use is scarce – they are all mined by hand - and they are therefore very expensive. On the other hand the crystals should be relatively straight forward to grow and easier to handle than quartz. As they have a wide frequency response they can also provide a reliable and readily accessible component suitable for many oscillators. This provides an alternative to the magnetostriction sets I design that generally use valve transmitters.

NRL and the Naval Radio and Sound Laboratory here in California are mainly concerned with research into high-frequency radio, underwater sound propagation and submarine warfare and this encompasses research and development of piezoelectric materials. It is these that I use when designing and developing direction finding devices and Asdic. At present NRL scientists work in conjunction with commercial companies - Bell Telephone Laboratories, a subsidiary of Western Electric Company, is the main one – because this collaboration is seen as the fastest, most effective, way to produce quick results in wartime.

The incentive for the commercial companies – and U.S. scientists - is the possibility of patents that may prove to be very profitable after the war. Unfortunately, employed by the Admiralty, we in Britain do not have the right to patent our work. Once I have learnt the U.S. crystal growing method I will be able to set up a similar production of ADP crystals for the Admiralty in Britain without having to go through the lengthy research and development already undertaken here. Even at this late stage of the war time is of the essence.

I find myself a houseguest of Ray, a Naval officer and his family and am very pleased not to be in an impersonal hotel. They are a charming family who are delighted to have an Englishman – I am flattered – as a guest. The house is spacious and has a large swimming pool in the garden although, disappointingly, it is too nippy to swim. Everything is extremely smart and comfortable compared to our flat in Largs. The scientists' standard of living here – their modern cars, the childrens' bicycles, their washing machines and refrigerators - is so much higher than that in Britain. And, compared with war torn London, it is wonderful to eat such a choice of foods and have beer and spirits on tap.

I explain about our food rationing at home and they say, "Oh, yes, we understand because we have rationing here too. Sugar is rationed and we have two meatless days a week". As I have eaten meat at every meal, every day, since I have arrived I am surprised and ask how that can be. "Well", they explain to me earnestly - with no sense of British irony – "to cope with our meatless days we buy extra rations of meat on our meat days!"

I am aware that Pratt is an experienced scientist but, lacking the specific chemical and technical knowledge necessary to interact with our American counterparts directly without having to explain details, it complicates matters. I do wonder if, wisely appreciating that this is not his area of expertise, he decides to leave shortly for Canada and I am better able to investigate their experimental methods and learn the techniques that they have found most successful more effectively.

After a few weeks I am thoroughly enjoying my time here both with NRL and Bell Tel (they love abbreviations) as the American scientists are such a friendly bunch. They work long and hard but they have a good family life and are more informal than my British colleagues. Within days of my arrival they dispense with Doctor Alexander and shorten my name to Alex. I am invited everywhere and it is very pleasant to meet and dine with their families. My only slight disappointment is that it is not as hot as I had hoped. Apparently San Diego is warm all year so it is unfortunate that I am visiting in November and December their coolest months. However, as it is nothing like as cold as Scotland, I am thankful for what warmth there is.

The civilian scientists involved in underwater sound research and development that I am working with here at Bell Tel are all very interested in our research and development in the U.K. and I am fascinated to see their labs and what they can achieve for telephony using ADP crystals in place of Rochelle salt. They in turn have found my take on things as a physical chemist very interesting as both sciences are central to acoustic research.

We exchange many ideas and agree that there is much to be gained from pooling information. They try to pick my brains about other research at Fairlie and my areas of special knowledge (the depth-determining asdic set, streamlined domes, torpedoes, sonobuoys) but I have to be very circumspect not to give any confidences away. The top scientists at Bell Labs and NRL are as smart (clever: I am picking up on Americanisms) as those I work with at Fairlie – quick witted, focused, scientifically qualified, technically able and inventive. To watch them as a group, discussing, writing on the blackboard and making calculations at amazing speed using their sliderules – or slipsticks as they call them – is very stimulating.

Working with these scientists and technicians is a wonderful experience for me and – should I succeed in growing synthetic crystals - one that the Admiralty should be pleased with. In turn, everyone here is keen that I visit again when this war is over as they say they would like to preserve and enlarge on the good working relationship that has built up with the scientists in the Admiralty and Royal Navy. Hopefully they consider the modest contributions I have made to their research here has been of benefit too.

The news that the Germans have broken through in the Ardennes means that the end of the war is not about to happen as we had all hoped. I am so looking forward to seeing Muriel but after the peace here I am not looking forward to more of the same in war torn Britain. But I have finally reached the point where I feel that I have gained all the knowledge I can and clearly understand the process and method they have developed for growing ADP crystals, well enough, at least, to design my own version. I therefore start to make arrangements to get back to Scotland. It is not going to be straightforward.

I fly from San Diego to Seattle then onto Ottawa in order to get a flight home to Prestwick. Sadly, once on the plane from Ottawa the weather is so terrible — heavy snow and ice — that we are forced to land in Newfoundland because visibility is so poor. The pilot is worried we will not make it across the Atlantic. Other planes have been diverted here too and under the circumstances I am very relieved to get into the only hotel available.

However, in the lobby, cold and tired, I am disappointed to find that it is impossible to buy a drink before dinner — the bar will not serve me a glass of whisky. Those Scottish settlers obviously brought their Protestant puritanism with them. I decide to visit the liquor store opposite the hotel for a small bottle of whisky to warm me up and calm me down. Unfortunately I find this is not simple either. The store owner insists that a customer cannot simply buy one bottle of whisky but has to buy a bottle each of three spirits - one gin, one vodka and one whisky - in order to get the desired bottle of whisky, so that is what I do, leaving the gin and vodka at the store to avoid unnecessary tax.

Having heard that on landing in the U.K. tax is not only payable on bottles of spirits but payable also on new stockings, back at the hotel I wash all 20 pairs of stockings and hang them over the bath to dry. They will then no longer be new. When the chamber maid comes to turn down the bed she looks very surprised indeed and eyes me askance. The next morning I hear that there is a plane due to leave so, leaving my breakfast unfinished, I hurriedly pack my belongings, leave a tip for the maid on my night stand and make off for the airstrip double quick.

No sooner than arriving, the flight is cancelled due to foul weather. Disappointed, I rush back to the hotel, secure the same room and am quickly able to retrieve the tip before the maid comes to make up the room. This happens twice more, each time my disappointment only slightly mitigated by my managing to retrieve the ever growing tip. Finally, both the maid and I get our just reward as, determined to get back in time for Christmas, I manage to talk my way onto the only plane flying to Prestwick, a Lancaster bomber converted by the Canadians for carrying troops across the Atlantic.

The plane is empty, not simply of the men it has flown here but even of seats. They have all been removed to give enough room for the troops and I too shall have to sit on the floor of the fuselage for the entire flight home. It looks far from comfortable but if I don't fly home in it I may be here for several more days. And travelling on that plane, the floor vibrating, the fuselage large and empty, the air so cold that my feet are lumps of ice, fingers frozen, with Michael's teddy bear stuffed into my jacket to act as insulation and my precious samples wedged between my knees I do everything I can to keep my thoughts focused, my mind alert and fears at bay.

Photograph of a Lancaster XPP in Canada

I go over all the mnemonics I used at school to pass my history exams, I try and recount the entire periodic table, every joint in the crayfish and, finally, I recite the poem I first read on the hills above Fairlie, a revelation to me then, almost a reality now, a reminder of all that I have seen in my life and pray to see again.

Much have I travell'd in the realms of gold,
And many goodly states and kingdoms seen;
Round many western islands have I been
Which bards in fealty to Apollo hold.
Oft of one wide expanse had I been told
That deep-brow'd Homer ruled as his demesne;
Yet did I never breathe its pure serene
Till I heard Chapman speak out loud and bold:
Then felt I like some watcher of the skies
When a new planet swims into his ken;
Or like stout Cortez when with eagle eyes
He star'd at the Pacific - and all his men
Look'd at each other with a wild surmise -
Silent, upon a peak in Darien.

Yes, I pray. Never religious, having spurned all of it as divisive, bunkum, unproved, unscientific, I pray to any powers that be that this rumbling, carcass of a plane will get me back across the ocean to Scotland so that my samples can be of use to our war effort and, if not in time for that, then able to be developed for all that will be to come when this war is over. Because we at the Establishment are all well aware that although this war is nearly over, it is only the beginning of a monumental era of technical and scientific research into weapons and counter weapons. It will be essential to build on this to make sure we are fully equipped should such a war happen again.

And becoming increasingly introspective and maudlin I make myself think of happier times, to my childhood, to the educational obstacles I eventually conquered and to all the wonderful places from Africa to England that I have visited and to those first memorable journeys with my parents. And, inevitably, I think of Muriel and trust that I will get back to her in one piece and, as promised, back in time for Christmas day together, to see the end of 1944 and to toast a better 1945.

Excerpt from *On First Looking into Chapman's Homer*, John Keats.

37. Johannesburg to Durban: South Africa, 1921 - 1925

Phil Alexander, 1925

The Umgeni River twists and turns through The Valley of a Thousand Hills before it gets to the sea. I was never sure — nor am I now — that there were ever that many hills and I always meant to find out. We often went through The Valley of a Thousand Hills for a spin in the car. Mom enjoyed it because she found it pleasantly cool after Durban and Dad always agreed to take us because it was not too long a drive for a day's outing.

As we motored along we could look down on the river from the loop road which ran along the ridge. Mom never failed to say how majestic that view was. The river looked like a great snake to me as it wound in and out along the valley floor and even the orange buds of the lilies that grew by the road reminded me of them. All of the flowers that grew there were very bright - exotic, Mom called them.

The road had so many bends that Dad was forced to drive very slowly and so I took it upon myself to describe things to him. Mom always worried he would crash if he looked at them and so would say, 'Hey, keep your eyes on the road, Philip', so I felt that Dad never had a chance to see the acacia trees and the vegetation and the wonderful view of the river that so awed Mom and myself.

I also remember spending a considerable amount of time looking up to spot kestrels out of the car window. Dad encouraged me to use the encyclopaedia to find out facts and, as he read it to me, together we learnt that as the air near the earth warmed it became thinner and lighter causing it to rise up in columns. The kestrels would soar over the cliffs on these warm currents of air on constant lookout for prey. Spotting a small mammal they would hover – flapping their wings very fast - until they dropped down onto it, tearing it to pieces. Like all bloodthirsty young boys I found that thrilling.

We usually took a picnic lunch along with us because Mom made such good ones. Crispy light sausage rolls or tasty chicken and ham patties which we ate with her date chutney. On the way back we would stop at a tearoom for Dad to 'stretch his legs' and for Mom to have a refreshing cup of tea. Inevitably I had a pineapple lemonade and a cake, usually most *bolletjes* with sugar on top. These outings left me with a warm feeling and I know I shall take outings like these when I have a family.

The valley is Zulu country now but the Debe tribe were there originally. The Zulus call the river Mngeni which means river of the acacia trees. They still live in their round grass huts and we would often see groups of them all dressed up in their colourful beads for a wedding or some other celebration. I would have liked to get out and speak with them – I liked to practice what Zulu I knew - but Mom would warn Dad not to slow down as she claimed that there were always fisticuffs, as she called it, when they had celebrations, and she insisted that we kept the windows wound up and speeded up. But when we stayed with our friends the Morrisons on their stud farm near Jo'burg I had plenty of opportunity to talk with the Zulu men as they sat around the camp fire, watching their women work.

When I was five years old we left Johannesburg (Mom had high blood pressure and suffered nosebleeds due it being 600 feet above sea level) for Durban, driving over the Drakensberg Mountains and then through the valley down to the coast. Dad drove an American Buick with running boards and wheels with wooden spokes and a nifty little windscreen wiper that the driver had to work by hand. Before we got in the car Mom would ask the gardener if the windscreen had been wiped. She was referring to his having to rub the whole windscreen with the cut side of a potato so the starch would stick to the glass and allow the raindrops to run off the windscreen.

However, after some time in the rain the potato starch wore off and the rain drops stuck to the windscreen so Dad had to wipe the windscreen himself using the wiper which, he said, was a real fag. A small wire came through the windscreen from the wiper blade and Dad would twist it left or right to make the wiper work which, although my parents thought it a bit of a palaver, I thought it a fascinating manoeuvre. A simple solution for a simple problem.

The Buick did not respond well to coming over the mountains – the Drakensberg mountains are over 10,000 feet - as the engine used to go 'pin, pin, pin' and slowly cough to a stop. It was called 'pinking' and occurred because the engine didn't get enough air into it due to the float chamber not being at the top. This meant that Dad would have to get out on the mountain and change the carburettor - which as Dad explained to me mixed air with the petrol - to cope with the change in altitude. Once Dad had learnt to recognise the problem he always altered these settings on the way down which made his life easier but I missed the bit of excitement that stopping and repairing the engine involved.

Living in Johannesburg I can clearly remember Dad cracking open huge wooden packing cases that had big square tins of petrol in. This was essential because they didn't have petrol stations in Jo'burg then although when we went back a year or two later they had begun to appear. To fill the car with petrol he had to siphon it which he did by putting one end of a tube into the petrol, sucking the other end of the tube until the petrol came up it. Before the petrol reached his mouth he quickly put the tube into the car petrol tank so the petrol ran from the big tank up the tube into the car. I could always imagine what would happen if he sucked too hard and got a mouthful of petrol. *Verrot.*

He also filled smaller cans to take with us in the car which I often helped him do. Lifting the big ten gallon tin whilst I held the funnel on legs to keep it still, he poured the petrol through a V shaped funnel into the smaller petrol tins. The locals all liked those petrol cans when they were empty as they cut the tops off and used them for cooking pots. They boiled their pap in them and also used them to make their beer drinks in. Nothing in Africa is wasted. I was allowed to have the packing case to make a camp as it was big enough for me and our pet Pekingese to get in but when I had tired of the game the staff took the packing cases home for firewood.

Eric, aged 5, 1921

The main roads in Jo'burg were all metalled by that time, their smooth surfaces a pleasure to drive on. But on the small side streets and on the roads around Durban they were still dirt roads. Driving along on an open road one could see if a car was coming from several miles off due to the dust. It was always my job to shout, 'Car Coming', and we would wind up our windows until it passed. Otherwise we would all be covered from top to toe in red dust.

Rain was another hazard after which the roads would be thick mud. On one occasion when we came from Jo'burg to Durban the mud was so deep that it rose right over the running boards and we had to be pushed back on the road. Mom swore then that that was the last time she would take that journey by road but that she would travel by train in the future. But we continued to go everywhere by car because Dad liked driving, and so did Mom. Happy memories.

38.   The End of It: Scotland, 1945

Staff at H.M. A/SEE, Fairlie 1945
Muriel sitting, 2nd row, 6th from right, Eric standing 3rd row, 22nd from right

Montgomery's forces crossed the Rhine at the end of March 1945 and at the end of April the Russians from the east and the Americans from the west met and Germany was divided into two. On 1st May the news broke that Hitler had killed himself and the next day the Germans surrendered in Italy, followed by the fall of Berlin. On 4th May German troops in Denmark surrendered and, although the Unconditional Surrender of German forces was signed on 4th May, news was still awaited in Britain that the war had finally come to an end.

On 7th May, still waiting for news, Eric and Muriel travelled over-night by train down to London on to the way to a week long holiday in Brighton, and missed the announcement. On 8th May they arrived in London – already packed with revellers - and had to queue for breakfast at Lyons Corner House on Piccadilly. There they bumped into Muriel's next door neighbour from Glasgow, James Beard, who described to them how the cease fire had begun when Germany unconditionally surrendered to the Western Allies at 2am.

Victory in Europe Day (VE Day), 8th May, was a day for celebrations all over the country. Churchill announced on the radio that "Hostilities will end officially at one minute after midnight today." there were rejoicing street parties, cheering crowds, patriotic marching groups of children and general enthusiastic flag waving and revelry. Ship sirens hooted and excited children lit Victory bonfires. Revellers danced and drank until the next morning.

When Muriel and Eric returned from their holiday, work at the Establishment over the next few months carried on much as before. Meanwhile, the war for British, Commonwealth and US forces continued in the Far East. After the Allies overcame the Japanese at Okinawa in June the war culminated on 6th and 9th August with the dropping of two atomics bombs by US forces at Hiroshima and Nagasaki. On 15th August, Imperial Japan surrendered to the Allies.

On the evening of Victory in Japan Day (VJ Day), 15th August, Eric, Muriel and Mrs Alexander dined with Muriel's friend Nessie Templeton and her parents at their house in Largs. To celebrate "Eric took a slug out of each bottle on the sideboard and mixed them cocktails and a very tiddly time was had by all". But Muriel suffered the next morning. It was not from the alcohol as she thought; she was pregnant with the first of their four children. With the signing of the surrender by the Emperor of Japan of 2nd September 1945, WWII officially ended.

With the war at an end, generally those working at Fairlie returned to civilian life and their previous employment and research at universities, experimental laboratories and commercial companies. Others returned to active service in the Royal Navy. Those who had come from the Admiralty Research Laboratory (ARL) Teddington, could return there although Vigoureux and Law – formerly of Portland - joined the Torpedo Experimental Establishment (TEE) in Greenock where Eric joined them to carry out torpedo research for a period of time. Brown returned to Cambridge University and the other Cambridge men (Astbury, Bacon, Fry, Fisher, Roberts) had similar avenues open to them: whilst most of those who had worked at Portland (Anderson, Colquhoun, Davis, Dawson, Hanley, Herbert, Jackson, Johnson, Morgan, Pew and Smith) returned there to H.M. Underwater Detection Establishment (HMUDE) when H.M. A/SEE closed down in February 1946.

Muriel continued working at Fairlie until October 1945 when, six months pregnant, she gave up her job. However Eric – who had joined the Admiralty research establishment immediately on gaining his doctorate – did not have any previous employment to return to. He had enjoyed the research he undertook during wartime and could envisage many interesting areas for research within the Admiralty scientific service. Now he had a family to provide for, he decided that the civil service could provide him with a secure career. However, to continue his research and stay employed by the Admiralty post-war it was necessary to apply and take the civil service exams like all civilians. He did so, coming first equal in chemistry, in the open competition of over 1000 applicants to join the Admiralty Royal Naval Scientific Service.

After the war Mrs. Alexander, Eric's mother, having spent the majority of the war living in London, accompanied her son and his wife to Dorset, returning to South Africa for a spell in 1947. Eric's cousin, Sara Miranda, returned safely from Egypt by ship in 1945 with five other women in the First Aid Nursing Yeomanry alongside over 90 British 'Palestinian Police'. Dom Mintoff, who was up at Oxford at the same time as Eric, became a Labour politician in his native Malta followed by Prime Minister in 1955; Moshe Feldenkrais, Eric's friend, developed an internationally accepted type of exercise therapy, known as the Feldenkrais Method, and emigrated to Israel.

When the war ended the United States Office of the Chief of Naval Operations noted, "*The terrific 72 months battle in which control of the seas was vitally essential to victory had cost the Allies about 4773 Merchant ships (21,141,000 gross tons) sunk by enemy action. During the war 996 Axis submarines were sunk, and 221 more plus scores of midgets were captured after enemy capitulations. Credit for sinking enemy submarines was assigned approximately to Britain for 70 per cent and to the United States for 30 per cent."*

In 2019 Wikipedia quotes: "The outcome of the battle was a strategic victory for the Allies—the German blockade failed—but at great cost: 3,500 merchant ships and 175 warships were sunk in the Atlantic for the loss of 783 U-boats (the majority being Type V11 submarines) German surface warships, including 4 battleships (*Scharnhorst, Bismarck, Gneisenau* and *Tirpitz*) 9 cruisers, 7 raiders, and 27 destroyers. Of the U-boats, 519 were sunk by British, Canadian, or other allied forces, while 175 were destroyed by American forces; 15 were destroyed by Soviets and 73 were scuttled by their crews before the end of the war for various causes."

U-boats sunk by the British were detected when submerged by the continually improving anti-submarine detection devices (Asdic) on board British vessels. The submarines were either torpedoed, hit by projectiles onboard the ships or rammed by them. Incontestably, the work of the scientists at H.M. Anti-Submarine Experimental Establishment in Fairlie, Scotland had been of paramount importance in fighting the U-boat threat and their resolute efforts had saved innumerable lives.

Muriel & Eric, Fairlie, Scotland 1945

39. Post WWII

HMS *Brocklesby*, Type 1 Hunt-class destroyer

"Sonar-Detector of Submerged Submarines," Lt. Cdr. A.P.Hilar, USN, Section Op413C4 of the Office of the Chief of Naval Operations and given to the Naval Office of Public Information for release to the Press on 6 April 1946. *"Early in 1939 it became apparent that training of personnel could not be handled as a by-product of engineering and tactical tests. Consequently the U.S. Fleet Sonar School at San Diego was established in order to increase training facilities. The Radio and Sound School of NRL also expanded its technical training in Sonar. ....To provide more equipment and training, the Radio Corporation of America was placed under contract by the Bureau of Ships and commenced production of echo ranging Sonar in the summer of 1939. The value of Sonar was becoming keenly appreciated."*

"Sonar and Asdic scientists became aware that they had parallel developments and possesses practically identical equipment. The primary differences were: British Asdic transducers contained quartz-

steel while U.S. Sonar had magneto-striction; British Asdic domes were streamlined while ours was a sphere; British Asdic ranges were permanently recorded on a range recorder while Sonar ranges were indicated on a dial.

The range recorders are a valuable aid in conducting an attack; we obtained samples from Britain and the Sangamo Electric Company started producing our own types. The streamlined dome increased the ships speed at which Sonar could be effectively operated from 10 up to 15 knots; we adopted it from Britain, Canada furnished some equipment, then The Submarine Signal Company; the Rice-Barton Company, and the E.G.Budd Company commenced production of U.S. equivalents.

Britain also furnished some Asdic Electronic Attack Teachers which provided realistic methods of manoeuvering models of an Asdic fitted escort attacking an evasive U-boat within the confines of a Sonar classroom. These Asdic Teachers added to the growing number of Sonar Teachers.

Thus began a technical liaison which quickly enveloped British Asdic and American Sonar scientists, officers, technicians, etc., into a family known to each other by first names."

Lt. Cdr. A.P. Hilar, USN

A rubber coating was fitted on to the outer hull of U-boats during 1943/44 and the US Navy, the British Navy and the Admiralty were concerned – after the unexplained sinking of several Allied vessels in 1944 and investigating a surrendered U-boat - that this synthetic rubber was so effective in deflecting sonar beams and dampening the sound of the submarine engine that hunting or deep diving U-boats would continue to go undetected.

The rubber, originally made into tiles 0.16 inch thick, was glued onto the outer surface of the submarine. However, the adhesive used to glue the tiles was not performing well as these tiles were apt to fall off and alternative adhesives and rubber coatings were researched in Germany – and in the US and UK – from 1944 onward. When the hostilities were over in 1945 Dr. Alexander was asked to travel to Gottingen and Hamburg in Germany on behalf of the Admiralty to investigate the latest improved synthetic rubber coating that had been applied successfully to the exterior of some U-boats which allowed them to avoid asdic detection and muffle underwater sound.

Dr. Alexander obtained samples and returned to Britain with them to undertake further analysis. The samples confirmed that the outer layer of the synthetic rubber sheet covering was smooth but an attached inner layer contained a series of voids - small regular perforations - which formed air pockets that absorbed specific sonar beams when they hit the rubber coating. Investigation also confirmed that the rubber layers approximately 4mm thick overall had the additional benefit that the sound of the U-boat's engine was also dampened.

U.S. Navy, Press Release on 6 April 1946. *"Research development, ideas, etc., were exchanged, U.S. observers were stationed at British Admiralty Anti-U-boat activities, Britain had representatives at U.S. Navy activities, both countries exchanged visits to laboratories, etc.*

A laboratory was established at San Diego under the University of California Division of War Research, and sponsorship of formal work at Woods Hole Oceanographic Institution was taken over. Several research groups were set up under Columbia University Division of War Research, including a Theoretical Analysis Group, The Underwater Sound Reference Laboratories, and a Sonar Laboratory at New London (resulting in the establishment of the USN Underwater Sound Laboratory, New London).... Prominent scientists, including Nobel prize winners, sought more effective means of finding submarines. Extensive experiments were tried off San Diego by the California Division of War Research ...these were unsuccessful and ....Scientific and engineering effort was thenceforth concentrated on further development of the Navy's existing underwater sound techniques. Britain contributed her entire history on scientific investigations of under-water sound".

Following his fact-finding visit to California in 1944 Dr. Alexander designed, set up and oversaw a relatively simple ammonium dihydrogen phosphate (ADP) crystal growing facility - run by Trevor Gulliwell - for the Admiralty in Redruth, Cornwall, following advice given by Bell Telephone Laboratories and Naval Research Laboratory in San Diego, USA. The ADP crystals were grown in a hydrothermal solution using a rocker mechanism – the movement needed to grow the crystals – and the resulting oscillators were produced in Bath.

It was essential that the synthetic quartz crystals produced were not 'dirty' - that they had the minimum imperfections - in order to be of high enough quality for use in British underwater sound projectors and hydrophones. The crystals took only months to grow, were cheap to produce and easier to handle than the more expensive and difficult to find, natural quartz crystal. As can be seen in Dr. Alexander's reports below, British ADP crystals for oscillators were available for experimental purposes by November 1946.

Below: Selection of Unclassified Reports 1946 by Dr. E.A. Alexander, HM Underwater Detection Establishment, (HMUDE) Portland, England.

'Electro-acoustic oscillators: Experimental quartz oscillator (15in diameter, 30, 65 kc/s). Establishment Report No. 2; June 1946 (Unclassified)'

'Electro-acoustic oscillators No.3: Multi-element quartz-steel oscillator. (A/S638, 21 in by ¾in, 50kc/s). Establishment Report No.9; November 1946 (Unclassified)'

'Electro-acoustic oscillators No. 5: Experimental A.D.P. oscillator (4¾ in by ¾ in, 100 kc/s). Establishment Report No.11; November 1946 (Unclassified)'

'Electro-acoustic oscillators No.11: Experimental A.D.P. line hydrophone in a parabolic reflector of aperture 23in by 10 ½ in. Establishment Report No.17; December 1946 (Unclassified)'

'Electro-acoustic oscillators No.7: Experimental A.D.P. oscillator (1 in by 1 in, 50kc/s). Establishment Report No.18; December 1946 (Unclassified)'

By the late 1940's the American term *transducer* replaced the British term *oscillator* and it was in the mid-fifties that the term *sonar* became widely used replacing the British term *Asdic*.

Below: Photograph of Chief Scientists at the dinner held at the Royal Hotel, Weymouth, 1952 to celebrate the Silver Jubilee of H.M. Underwater Detection Establishment, Portland.

Sitting from left:
Mr J. Anderson CBE; Dr D. Tucker; Mr B. Smith OBE; Mr A. Main;
Mr W. Cook CB MSc; Mr A. Law; Alderman Medlam Mayor of Weymouth;
Capt R. Portlock OBE RN; Capt G. Sayer DSC RN; Mr H. Kenny MBE;
Capt S. Boord RN; Rear Adm H. Morse RN, DSO.
Standing from left:
Dr W. Jackson; Mr G. Hales; Mr A. Pew OBE; Capt E. Bayldon DSC RN;
Dr E. Alexander; Cdr N. William-Powlett DSC RN; Mr D. Handley;
Capt R. Dendy; Lt Cdr C.R. Sims RN; Mr J. Coloquhoun;
Capt A. Forman DSC RN; Dr Joe Fisher; Lt Cdr A. Hilar USN.

Throughout the 1950's Dr. Alexander and the other scientists at HM Underwater Detection Establishment liaised and worked with American scientists at Portland, England. Many of the American scientists worked for US Naval Establishments in the USA and came over to the UK with their families for tours of duty. Lt. Cdr. A.P. Hilar, USN, visited – and was possibly seconded to – HMUDE, England after the war. He is shown in the photograph celebrating 25 years of the Establishment in 1952.

In addition scientists from HMUDE continued to work with American Naval scientists and with Bell Telephone Laboratories in the US regarding sound research. Underwater weapons trials were carried out together at US Naval Facilities in the Bahamas where suitable sites exist as the continental shelf drops steeply onto the Atlantic ocean floor with its extremely cold currents. Similar acoustic surveys and sonar ship and towing trials were carried out with the US Navy and the Royal Navy off Gibraltar. The Asdic set Type 177 was trialed there on Captain John Crawford's vessel, HMS *Brocklesby*.

In the mid 1950's Dr. Alexander was head-hunted by 'Bell Labs' to work for them in America doing sound research. Bell would pay for his family to be relocated but with highly interesting research to undertake for the Admiralty, a good Civil Service pension, a National Health Service and four children to educate, he declined the offer.

With the advent of superior atomic powered submarines - which could spend long periods of time submerged at increasing depths and travel at increasing speeds, able to be launched from anywhere at any time – some of the anti-submarine detection devices for submerged submarines developed during the war were becoming out-moded although certainly not all of them.

The mechanical model of the British up-turned echo sounder developed by Dr. Alexander was installed in the US nuclear submarine *Nautilus* to determine when it was under the ice cap during its north polar journey.

The following article on the journey of submarine *Nautilus* was written by Dr. Alexander, published with the encouragement and approval of the Admiralty in the *Young Scientist - A Supplement to Research*, Butterworth Scientific Publications, London 1958, p 31 - 34.

"UNDERNEATH THE POLAR ICE-CAP", E.A. Alexander.

"An achievement such as the passage of the sub-marine 'Nautilus' underneath the north polar ice cap takes one's mind back to the arduous journey of that great Antarctic explorer Robert Scott and the quotation from his farewell letters "....how much better it has been than lounging in too great comfort at home". Surely this is a reminder of the tremendous advance of science in the last fifty years; to be able to glide smoothly under the North Pole with all modern conveniences – electric cookers, automatic washing machines, sun-lamps, daily cinema, a juke-box playing almost 24 hours a day, a Coca-Cola machine delivering iced drinks and air conditioning with a room temperature of 72 degrees F. All this gives quite the wrong impression; for a journey like this could never have been undertaken without careful planning and meticulous attention to detail.

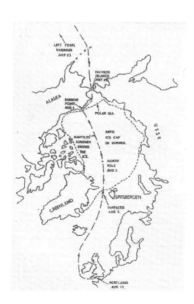

Figure 1. A map showing the route followed by the submarine 'Nautilus' from Diomede Islands (29th July) to a point between Greenland and Spitsbergen (5th August) underneath the polar ice cap.

241

It is known that the north polar ice cap is only a relatively thin scum of ice, rarely thicker than 12 feet. Aerial photography showed that the ice cap is broken up in summer into numerous patches of open water and cracks, and in winter is seldom without temporary regions of open water or very thin ice. The sea beneath lies in a deep basin, broken by occasional 'hills and ledges'. It must have been apparent for some time that a journey under the ice cap was feasible, but conventional-type submarines would not have sufficient endurance, whereas the nuclear submarine provides the perfect vehicle. The 'Nautilus' ventured under the ice cap between Greenland and Spitsbergen (see Figure 1) in the summer of 1957. In this exploratory voyage she travelled more than 1000 miles, approaching to within 180 miles of the pole. (A photograph of the submarine cruising on the surface is shown in Figure 2.) A great mass of scientific data was obtained, numerous soundings were taken and experience was gained concerning the behaviour of navigational equipment in the polar regions.

Figure 2, a photograph of the 'Nautilus' cruising on the surface

In February 1958, 'Nautilus' went into New London to undergo a complete overhaul to prepare for the polar journey. Any one of a number of things could go wrong and 'Nautilus' would be left hopelessly trapped under the ice cap with no chance of rescue. The nuclear reactor might fail leaving the ship to struggle along for a while on storage batteries. The navigational equipment could err leading the ship round and round in a slow circle, indicating all the time that she was travelling in a straight line. A disastrous fire could fill the ship with smoke; to guard against this, outlets to the main air supply were installed in all compartments and every man provided with an individual tube and mouthpiece to plug in and so obtain an independent supply of air.

On completion of this work 'Nautilus' headed for the west coast and berthed at Seattle in June. Here the Captain, Commander ANDERSON, was joined by a physicist from the Naval Electronics Laboratory and together they flew to Alaska from where they carried out an aerial reconnaissance of the Bering Strait. The Strait was clear and the ice cap well off shore, so they hurried back to join the ship. During the weeks steaming to the Strait, great changes were occurring in the Polar Sea. Enormous ice floes were breaking off the shore of the Canadian Arctic Archipelago and when the submarine slipped under the edge of the ice a great barrier of ice floes had drifted across her path. After proceeding 30 miles the sonar equipment detected masses of ice projecting downwards to a depth of 80 feet and only 80 feet of water remained below the ice. As 'Nautilus' is 50 feet from keel to periscope she was forced to turn back. She tried repeatedly to get through, but after three days abandoned the attempt and headed for Pearl Harbour. Next the navigating officer flew to Alaska and carried out aerial reconnaissance over the Strait and up the arctic coast to Barrow Point.

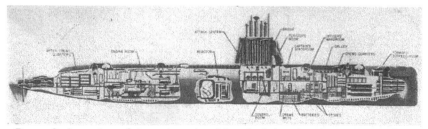

Figure 3. A section of the submarine 'Nautilus' showing the position of the engine room, nuclear reactor, the control rooms and the living quarters.

Finally on 23rd July 'Nautilus' slipped out of Pearl Harbour and travelled practically the whole way to the Bering Strait underwater, pushing out her radar antenna for only 30 seconds as she entered the strait on 29th July to take her last fix on Diomede Island. From then on she was cut off from the outside world with no sun, stars or radio stations to fix her position *(see Figure 4)*.

AIDS TO NAVIGATION

The '*Nautilus*' was fitted with various sonar and visual aids to navigation – an echo-sounder to determine the depth of the water below the keel, and up-turned echo-sounder to measure her distance from the ice above and a sonar set to explore the path ahead (Figure 4). In the continuous daylight the under surface of the ice could be constantly observed with a television camera. Due to the pressure of winds and currents, ice in the arctic basin often forms downward projections 50 feet deep and sometimes considerably more. A continuous record of the profile of the under surface of the ice was taken during the journey and the position of every patch of clear water plotted, for surfacing in an emergency.

This time '*Nautilus*' detoured from the direct northern approach to the Arctic basin and headed down into the Barrow Point sea valley which flanks the northern Alaskan coast. At first the valley is about 300 feet deep and 4 to 5 miles wide but gradually deepens to 1200 feet and widens to 10 to 12 miles. On reaching Barrow Point the submarine turned northwards and passed under the ice cap 12.37 G.M.T. on 1st August. The rest of the journey was made at a depth of 400 feet and a speed of 20 knots. Only once, during the second day under the ice, did she encounter the unexpected. The sonar set detected a steep underwater ridge directly across her path. Speed and depth were immediately reduced. Fortunately after a short while it was observed that the ridge stopped rising and began to level off. From then on the problem of navigation became more serious as the ship approached the pole. It is possible for a submarine to use a simple magnetic compass by placing the sensitive element at the top of the periscope to remove it as far as possible from the effect of the metal hull, but it would be of little use in this region due to violent perturbations in the earth's magnetic field.

One of the most important navigational devices is the gyroscope which is used in all major vessels. A 'free' gyroscope maintains its spin axis by pointing in a fixed direction in space and must be given some 'earthly' reference before it can be used as a compass. In a gyro-magnetic compass the earth's magnetic field is used as a reference and hence near the pole it suffers from the same effects as the magnetic compass. In a gyro-compass, however, the earth's gravitational field is used as a reference. Hence it is a true north-seeking device independent of magnetic phenomena. The gravitational control results from the tilt of the spin-axis caused by the earth's rotation, but at the pole a tilt of the axis is not produced by the earth's rotation. As the gyro-compass approaches the pole, due to frictional effects, etc, it becomes more and more inaccurate and if it remained at the pole it would soon lose all sense of direction.

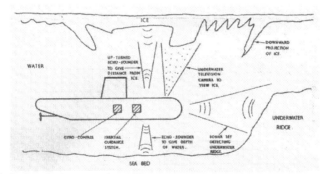

Figure 4. A sketch showing the different navigational devices which were used by 'Nautilus' to detect the underwater ridge and to ascertain her distance from the sea bed and the ice.

Fortunately the 'Nautilus' was also fitted with an inertial guidance system which was developed for missiles. This system is not bothered by any peculiar effects at the pole and consists mainly of two accelerometers. Presumably this 'black box' measures the accelerations in the horizontal plane in two directions mutually at right angles to each other and processes these measurements to obtain the distance and direction travelled in unit time. What must have been in doubt, however, was the degree of accuracy that could be achieved by the system, and this is covered by Commander Anderson's own words 'I was sceptical about the inertial gear, at first, but I must say I am amazed at its accuracy'. The data from this system was used by the navigating officer in the vicinity of the pole as a reference for the gyro-compass which controlled the autopilot.

On Sunday, 3rd August, 'Nautilus' passed under the North Pole; the depth of the water was 13,410 feet and its temperature 32degrees F. The only break in the routine was for a moment of silent prayer and a hush fell over the ship as she glided silently onwards. The North Pole is not the middle of the arctic ice cap and therefore more than half the journey under the ice had been completed. Furthermore, the route which lay ahead was already known from the reconnaissance of the previous year.

'Nautilus' emerged from under the ice cap and surfaced on the Greenwich meridian at 79degrees North at 13.54 G.M.T. on 5th August. She had travelled 1830 miles under the ice in 97 hours – a truly remarkable feat. How closely her actual position on surfacing agreed with her predicted position is probably a secret. Anyway, we can rest assured that navigation under the polar ice cap has been mastered, as can be judged by the smoothness with which the second nuclear submarine 'Skate' repeated the journey.

Until now the submarine has been an improvisation which could never have had even the remotest commercial value. But who knows what future lies in store for the submarine cargo ship, for the feats of the nuclear submarine have surpassed man's dreams of a north-west passage.

Figures 2 and 3 are reproduced from official photographs by kind permission of the United States Navy."

"Underneath the Polar Ice-Cap", E.A. Alexander.

"Until now the submarine has been an improvisation which could never have had even the remotest commercial value. But who knows what future lies in store for the submarine cargo ship, for the feats of the nuclear submarine have surpassed man's dreams of a north-west passage." From this observation in the article written by Dr. Alexander in 1958 it is possible that at that time the full commercial future of nuclear submarines and their sonar was not foreseen.

In fact, the research and improvements made to sonar technology during and immediately after the war years contributed enormously to the commercial success of sonar today where it is used, among other things, to map the ocean floor, locate underwater hazards and find sunken wrecks. In addition, sonar devices facilitate the laying of cables across the seas, identify the movement of underwater mammals and locate shoals for the fishing industry. And, increasingly, sonar technology is used in our everyday lives such as the sonar sensors that are in active use in cars to aid reversing and parking. All of these are of great commercial value.

Navy ships still rely on active sonar to detect submerged submarines and they have multiple detection devices fitted on their hulls. Sonar arrays are towed behind naval vessels to detect submerged submarines whilst sonobuoys are a vital detection device that beam up signals to aircraft. Submarines continue to use active sonar – although preferring passive sonar where detection is likely – and the sonar room in ships and submarines remains of prime importance.

Few people appreciate that underwater acoustics and many anti-submarine detection devices used today, on board ship and submarine alike, are based on British Asdic technology developed, modified and improved during the Second World War. And it is rarely appreciated – because it is a little known fact – that to a great extent this was accomplished by sonar scientists, engineers and technicians who were employed by the British Admiralty to work at Her Majesty's Anti-Submarine Experimental Establishment in Fairlie, Scotland in order to overcome the terrifying threat of the German U-boat.

Printed in Poland
by Amazon Fulfillment
Poland Sp. z o.o., Wrocław

61606631R00150